Growing Up Under

Giuidre's River Bend.

Books by the same author.

Primrose and friends.
Don't look back.
Simon's Story.
The Greenhouse Village.
John Tomlinson's Bookshop
A Variegated Community.
Our Years of Carefree Days.

Chapter 1.—Liela.

Angels are bright still, though the brightest fell.
Wm. Shakespeare.   Macbeth.

He felt quite content; his orange offshore jacket and scarf, his warm blue watch cap, his jeans chucked into white deck rubber boots; he had a stick in his hands that he cut a long time ago in the woods close to where he lived in that long time passed; the light rain was welcome; spring was not here yet, but the softness of the rain bore promise. He kept a look out for Jess, his one-year old Springer pup; Jess liked the walk, plenty of new smells, more and different from yesterday, but he remained in view of his friend Sam, he wouldn't want to lose him. And so, they went on together; Sam with his limitless view of his world and Jess; sifting through whatever filled his doggie mind on that day. On that day Sam's mind was a good mind, shuffling over the pages in the book that made up his life; emerging from school life, nobody knew what might come from the those decisions; but there was a lucky strike, only because it was popular in those times; he studied computer science; well, that was the step for all that came next. He got a job and soon was laid off; he got another break: another job, but only as a remote worker, for a company who might go under next week. But because, of Sam's efforts, and other free-spirited workers like him, the company did not go under, not next week or any other week; and all of the worthless share charts too that were provided, in those days of imminent chasm, instead of real wages, became real. The chasm became less, but Sam, one day in a moment of perplexes, sold his shares. Not a good design nor a bad one, they would have been worth more now, but not very much and he was happy with his bank balance.

So now he and Jess lived together, in what seemed like a magic place for the both of them.

In those early days Sam used to sail with a number of friends; three had their own boats and the rest crewed for them; there he was, a little sailor in the little sailing club; there was another group of sailors who had boats that were larger; these boats: both large and small joined together for a regatta three times a year; so the crews sailed the course and shared the beer had some kindship. So, time passed and the group of skippers from the large vessels got together as a group to venture to go to California to work: they rushed about, selling their flats, cars and much

else no longer required. One day, Michael, one of the big boat owners came to Sam over a beer. "Sam," he said, "of all you sailors here I would rest content if you were to have my boat. I'd like you to buy it from me."
Sam did not know how to answer Michael. "I'm sorry Mike, there's no way I could pay for your boat, no way, even though I do like it."
Michael smiled. "No, you don't understand, with this move to the coast there is lots of loss leaving stuff behind, but the new business will take care of that. I have the yacht with a broker but, frankly, it is a sad thing; so, I have decided to leave it to somebody who would care for it; and of all the sailors I know you are the one."
"I'm sorry Mike, I do like your boat very well, but there's no way I can pay for it, no way."
"No, that's not the deal, you can have the boat for ten cents on the dollar, she can be yours for $10,000. What do you think?"
So that evening, with Sam's bank envelope in his hand Michael signed the Documentation Certificate and Sam had a new life.
The next day, by mid-morning, Sam was driving toward the house where the boat, 'Liela' lay on her moorings. The house was close to the water, it was called River Bend House; and as he got out of the car, he could see the boat. But he had more important things to do. The house was well built,

but now the effect of years of unhurried neglect could be seen; the garden was not tended and the house itself could need some repair and some paint. He stood there looking around and wondering; what the custodian could say there, and what that could mean for him and his boat, still, have to pay his visit and see what might come from that. He knocked on the door, a lady opened it and said right away, “are you a friend of Michaels?”

“Well, yes I am.”

“Well, come on in, come on in, we’ll have a cup of tea, shall we? My name is Giuirdre”

So, Sam went in and sat at the kitchen table. Giuirdre put the kettle on and got the tea pot and tray into position. “Always make loose tea in a china pot, no good spending time with those bags, I get my tea in pound lots from a dealer in Boston; you’ll see, Michael did not see, not at that first time, but in time he grew to like it.”

So, they sat at the table, waiting for the tea to brew.

“Actually,” said Sam, “I bought Michaels boat and I have come to ask if I can keep it at your dock like Michael did.”

“Oh, I know that, Michael called me and told you were coming, you see, I know you might like his boat, but Michael thought it would be a good thing for the both of us. Me being the full tea drinker and all."

She smiled at him and Sam's inhibitions faded. Sam thrust on with the thoughts he had, previously, kept to himself.

"I thought, Giuirdre, that I might sell my flat in town and live out here on the boat. I thought that if you wanted a gardener to get all your flower beds and vegetables in order, well, we could share the produce; and, well, I could do most of the work on the house, woodwork repair and fresh paint, we could have a sort of commune, and well, we could be good for each other, I have no friends and I would be happy to spend my time this way.

But thus it was, when he got down to it, but much more than putting his flat for sale; when he got down to it he discovered that it was not really taking his stuff to the boat, it was much more like getting rid of his stuff and starting over. So, books, bedclothes, his clothes, most of his kitchen stuff, DVDs all to go; only his work stuff remained with the internet space he acquired for his work. He moved it all to the boat and blended it all with kitchen stuff so he could do the cooking that he always did. The apartment cleared and settlement next week he was ready to move.

He made a lot of purchases of gardening tools and took them with the rest of his stuff; he knocked on Giuirdre's door and told he was there and he brought some new tools for the gardening work that he began to begin next day, so; would Giuirdre be ready to be the boss over this work? Oh, and he had some dinner ready to would it be all right if he brought it up about six-o-clock for them to share. Oh; it didn't take much more for him to say "OK' he'll be back and he went off to his boat.

It was, for him, a long and laborious labor of love between of contentment and readjustment, lasting several months, for him to get the boat and his belongings in a shape for him to be familiar with; but, it was a period of nesting into a new life, a life previously he didn't know existed. But tonight, he made a leek pie ready to cook, cooked some asparigus and let that grow cold, got three kinds of cheese and some apples, a bottle of white wine, already cold and a bottle of Calvados. He gathered this all into a canvas bag with a bottle opener and white napkins and wound his way up the garden to Giuiurde's house. She met him at the door with a blank look at all his equipment but led the way to the kitchen. Sam laid his canvas bag on the table and got out his equipment. "So," he said, "this is our dinner; he laid out the cheese board with the fruit to be pealed later; the Calvados and the tiny glasses for our after dinner relax, some cold asparagus for our pie, which I will

now bake in your oven; and, while we wait, a cool white wine to begin. What do you think?"
"That's an endearing thing to do, Sam. I'm well, endeared!"
"Well, Michael told me if I brought you wine and food, why there was a fine chance to, you know, to know you even better. Well, that's what he said."
"You lie white man, be better to open the wine and be prepared for the baking to be done."
The evening drew on; the wine bottle was drawn deep by the time the leek pie was on the plates with the asparagus, the wine tasted well with the leeks, eggs and sauce; conversation was varied, the wine bottle lasted until the cheese plate was deployed. At last they lay back in the settee and had the Calvados go to bring on later dreams; Giuirdre had a second glass when Sam washed up and dried all the dishes and put all his stuff in his canvas bag. He stopped and learned over to give Giuirdre a little kiss and said he would see her on the morrow.
And thus, their lives moved on.
Tomorrow he began by showing Giuirdre a color chart and asked her to choose a color for the outside of her house. "I shall have to paint the two front windows before we plant the flowers, but meanwhile I can get the flowerbeds cleared and we will have a lovely time at the garden

center buying all the flowers that you have chosen. I shall start by getting all the flower borders ready and get the windows painted, then we can together, plant the flowers, but you have to keep them watered."

Later that day he came and sandpapered the two windows and the front door, and, dusted them off and painted them with a colored paint. "That's the primer," he told Giuirdre, "that's colored with some of the real paint, there should be time to put that on tomorrow."

Tomorrow came and the final coat was applied, and Sam brought Giuirdre out for inspection. "Very good!" She exclaimed, "how nice it will be to have it all like that."

Sam went off on more errands and came back with six bags of gravel for the paths and a square of shingles for the garden shed roof. He wasted no time in removing the old shingles and taping tar paper and then the new shingles in place. He begun sandpapering and painting and the old garden shed regained its glory. Then he layered the gravel where Giuirdre would use the path and she came out at the end of the day to inspect. She turned back into her house with a sniffle.

After four trips to the garden center they were pretty happy with the flower beds, Giuirdre was entranced and told Sam how lovely it would be to watch the flowers grow throughout the summer. But Sam was unmoved.

A week and a half later a truck pulled up and Sam went out to meet them.

"Right here, simple job, right across the garden shed roof."

And Sam's truck had brought a retractable awning, with electric cord, a wind gust shutter and a shade awning to wind down. It all was installed quickly and they took away their packing. Sam went to his boat dock for the antique metal table and the swing set and single chair. All put in place and he went away for Giuirdre to wake from her siesta.

Later, she called him on his phone and he went up to the house. She was sat in the swing-set rocking and crying. "You can't go on doing this, you just can't; but, this is just beautiful, it really is; come and sit by me, look at the flowers, the view of the river."

"The swing-set is for sitting in peace, or, it is long enough for you to lie on. The awning will keep the sunshine off you, the roll down shade at the end if you need it, and the awning can be set half way out if that suits you. I want it to be for you to really enjoy your flowers."

So, the summer wound its way towards fall; Sam did get the old kitchen garden into a preliminary shape by renting a rototiller and the ground was in good enough shape for the first year's vegetable planting.

He made an appointment and took Giuirdre for a nice couple of hours haircut at a spa, he got her appointments for her dentist and doctor and felt good about that. He took her into town to meet with a group of friends she was once a part of, and on those occasions, he took his lap top to the offices of his employer; it was an opportunity to coordinate with his boss and work there until it was time to take Giuirdre home again.

The weekly dinners continued; through the late summer and the fall they would meet at the table under the sunshade, but as the temperature fell, they moved into the kitchen again. One night, after they had sat back to relax Giuirdre said to him.

"You never seem to have a lady friend; is there some reason in your past for this Sam?"

"No, not really; I never have been a part of any organization, or group, or even any informal gathering; I never have had the chance to meet any lady friends and now living on the boat I am quite content."

"Well, the day after tomorrow you can come up for a coffee at lunch time and you can meet one of my friends – Gabriella, a friend from long ago, the daughter of a friend – now you promise to come – all right?"

The day after tomorrow Sam duly went up the path to meet Gabriella. They were introduced by Giuirdre and shook hands and smiled. Then Sam looked down.
"You have a Springer! And I can see that she's pregnant! Well, can I have one of the pups?"
Gabriella glanced at Giuirdre who nodded faintly.
"Yes, you can have one, you are the second person who have asked me and I have said yes to. Which do you want a dog or bitch?"
"Oh, it doesn't matter, but if I have choice a dog; then I will call it Jess."
So a new promise for Sam; he now had to make the boat a home for two; that was a lot to think about: a dog bed on the settee, but that would be for later when it was bigger; for now a dog bed that could be in the main cabin when he was there, move it to the aft cabin and something in the cockpit. This was a very, very something that was coming.
About eight weeks on he had a trip with Giuirdre to Gabriella's house to see the pups, there were five and he patiently studied them as they lived their little family lives with their siblings and their mother. He loved them all, but in the end, he chose a dog that held himself aloof from the others, not aloof perhaps but just a little more independent.

"That's Jess, my dog. Will you take care of him until I can take him home?"
Another four weeks and Gabriella brought him to Sam and said that before she could leave him, she had to inspect Jess's new home, she did and was well pleased with the dog beds, the bedroom and all other things Sam had brought. She gave Jess a kiss and left him there.
Sam began a month's work; the time to do his work and the time to begin to train Jess. To begin with he didn't get much success about 'no touch'; Jess could not keep from enthusiastically licking and fighting with the hands that had replaced Gabriella's. So, Sam concentrated on 'stay' and 'stay put'. So, at the end of a month Jess would stay, reluctantly, with one finger poised and 'stay put' was long range version of the same. He moved on to walking to heel and don't touch new people unless you are asked to. But together they grew together, as a team, a little team on the boat.
Giuirdre asked Sam and Jess to lunch one day to meet "someone else about dogs". On that day they went up to the house, Jess on his best red lead. Giuirdre introduced them to Nina, the first person to ask Gabrielle for a puppy; and she was there in the kitchen, with her dog Tina. There they sat: Giuirdre in charge and the dog people and

their dogs trying to be well behaved. Finally, Giuirdre said laughing.
"You two take those dogs for a walk, I didn't ask you here to drink tea, I asked you two see the dogs now they have gone from their family and to see how you are looking and being with them, so go; come back and give me a story of the two dogs."
Nina and Sam went off together and they walked for an hour or so and when they came back Sam invited Nina to the boat. He explained how Jess and he got along and how Jess and he lived. This is the saloon, we cook and eat in here, in the forward cabin are my lap top and whatever I need for my work; my bedroom is aft of the cockpit and to get into it I have to go out into it from the cockpit; later version of my boat have a walkway under the cockpit, but I like this better; so bedtime Jess and I go there. So, will you have tea with me?"
They shared their tea at the little booth, one each side of the table, with their dogs asleep on the floor.
"Giuirdre tells me you have no lady that visits you", said Nina, "and why would that be, a nice boat like this, no annoyances from others, a peaceful place. So why would that be?"
"I have never had a lady who wanted to be with me."

"Never ever had one?"
"No, not one, not any, ever."
"I find that very hard to believe, not one? Well I never. Do you not want one? You seem very happy with my company, me, the dogs, conversation; and really, from my point of view you are a very generous man with the things you do for Giuirdre."
"I like the things that I do for Giuirdre and I must say that the things I have done for Giuirrde have brought me satisfaction also."
So, my no-woman man, would you like some-one to be with you, now and again? I can't stay tonight but I will call you soon and we can have an evening together, just you and me and the dogs. How about that?"
"I'd like it very much."
Just after the weekend Nina called.
"Tomorrow night, no-women man. Will you make me one of the complex and mythical dinners that Giuirdre told me about; would you do that for me?"
"I'll do my best; compound but simple, delightful and nice wine. Dinner will be ready at seven."
It was just at seven, Nina and Tina on the dock. Sam pulled the boat close and they got on board.
"Shall we have dinner first and then take the dogs for a run." Asked Nina.

"Yes, that will be fine; so, come on down; the dogs can be together on the sole, we can start dinner." Nina took her place at the diner booth; Sam poured a glass of wine and got a brought in a plate of the smoked salmon and brie bread and rolled cheese bits.

"We can have some wine and munch these multifarious, delectability's; when I make dinner for Giuirdre these make the start of whatever conversation she had in her mind. Many times, I learn a lot about things I never knew existed; then, as things usually went, the second half of the wine went with the hot things that are in the oven. Tonight, so I can know more about you, the hot things are multi-variable bruschetta with coverings that you might not like, some with coverings that you will recognize, and well, some to go with the wine."

The evening began with wine, food and conversations mostly following the lead provided by Nina. They sat; Nina providing all the chatter, the new subjects, to talk over how was Giuirdre, how was the training with Jess going on, how was the training with Tina getting on: until it was time for Sam to get up and go to the oven. He got back into the conversation, a bit, and put the hot things out on plates and poured more wine. So, with the hot bruschettas: sardines, anchovies, bacon, clams, singeing their fingertips, a bit more wine and a becalming of Sam's troubled innocence, their evening drew on to Sam's washing the dishes as Nina talked to him, and then to a final coats on to take the dogs for their last walk. When they got back to the boat Sam said we might as well go in the aft cabin, get the dogs all settled, and - - - - .

So, they all four went to the aft cabin and closed the hatch and turned the heater down low; they got the dogs settled and then Sam looked lost.

"You go first," said Nina, "you go first and sit up and watch me get ready to come and join you."

He did; and he watched, and watched and watched until she climbed on the bed and under the clothes.

"Get the light," Nina said now, "get the light and we lie here together and touch hands and wonder about the future."

They did; they held hands for the longest time; and the future looked very bright for Sam. The hand holding and talking went on for a good while; but eventually Nina put the light back on to look at her slender brown boy with Giuirdre's garden leanness and brownness of body; and a virgin appetite for her. So, the handholding moved, slowly but steadily until, at some point in the small hours of the morning, they both lay back again holding hands once more.

Nina slept, but Sam did not. He lay with his head on the pillow looking at her; the short black hair, all crumpled now but with little waves all along her face, the little sun lines, so clear with her eyes closed, the nose and mouth all there, all so lovely, but would he be her man? Would he? - - would - - woul - - ? and he drifted off to sleep as well.
In the morning Nina gave him a long kiss and said she would call again soon.
And she did, maybe five or six times each month, not saying what controlled her choice, but always full of joy and consistency of her affection for him. So, Sam was content, well, not content; he would like to have married her, but content for the life he had now; Nina, Jess, Giuirdre, Tina, the boat, his job; what more could her have.
He had an individual life, one day he went for the groceries to make a dinner with Giuirdre and later in the week he went to groceries for a dinner he could make for Nina. In between he made a weekly trip to the wine shop to look around and find something new. He always bought a case and had a chat with the exotic owner and always bought a state lottery ticket just to be a hopeful. Once he had won $3.50 and bought a new toy for Jess; always he sat with Jess on his side on the seat of the car and he would always tell Jess he was trying for a new toy. Today he put the case of

wine on the floor and gathered up Jess in his seat belt.
"OK, today Jess, another new toy for you? "
He scratched away at the coating to read the number. He looked at the number, he looked back at his number, he looked at the real number.
"My goodness Jess we won a big one." He looked again. "My goodness Jess we have won $750,000!" He looked at the wrapper. Aghast, he didn't know what to do or think, all that money, what to do? What must I do? What must I do with it?
What about Nina? What about Giuirdre? He looked at the wrapper of the ticket; so, tomorrow we have to go to the State Lotteries Resource Center. I shall have to search myself about this Jess, I shall have to learn about this - - and tax paid Jess! What do you think of that?
The next morning Sam and Jess drove to the Resource Center. Sam left Jess in charge of the car and went in. It was, for a big winner, a bit of a let-down. An official took the ticket and made his way to whatever place it was that verified it and then he came back to say it was real and what did Sam want to do next. Sam said he wanted the award to be private and he wanted the money deposited in his bank; and here were the account numbers. This all took very little time and he was back with

Jess in short order. They went for a walk for Jess to be happy and then back in the car to go home. "Jess, I'm not very sure about all this, I have a feeling this might have been bad, but I don't know what to do about it; we'll let it grow a little hair and think about it."

But, like all of the rest of us, he let it drift into the background of his life and forgot about it.

Late fall now; Sam and Nina had plans to spend two winter evenings with Giuirdre; as time drew on into December, they fixed the dates; there would be two dates when the two of them spent the afternoon and evening with Giuirdre and two days when Sam would be there. Christmas day came and went, Giuirdre was away for a long weekend with her daughter. Then there was a New Year's party with Giuirdre, Nina and Sam; and then the January weather took hold of them for a while.

February turned mild and Sam took Jess out before breakfast, after lunch time and before bed. One lunchtime Sam was walking back to the house, Jess didn't want a leash for this walk and scurried back and forth on his own, but not too far away. This day, as they opened the gate into the back-yard Jess set up a frenzied barking and ran towards the house, Sam followed him and he found Giuirdre lying in the gravel path, very still. "Giuirdre, Giuirdre," he shouted at her, but she did not move; he touched her hand but it felt cold. He rushed into the house for several blankets and made her comfortable then called the ambulance. He was still there holding her in his arms when they arrived.

"You found her this way?" Asked the medic.

"No, actually my dog found her, but for him she could be still here. Will you take her to St Vincent's?"

"Yes, will you come along?"

"I'll drive my own car, but I had better go and get her address book for the family and all that."

The ambulance left and Sam found Giuirdre's phone book, and checked for her sister's number and then drove off to the hospital. He parked in the 'Emergency' car park and ran inside, he asked where incoming patients came in and got there in time to see the ambulance men transfer her to the hospital staff.

"No good now, my friend," said one of the medics, "you'll have to wait her for the nurse to come out."

Sam sat down and using Giuirdre's book called the daughter he had never met.

"Joyce? Is this the daughter of Giuirdre? Well, my name's Sam, I live on the boat as Giuirdre's; I found her this morning, well, my dog did; anyway, she was unconscious; I called the ambulance and they brought her to St Vincent's. I don't know anything and I don't expect to because I'm not a family, or so the ambulance medic told me. I'll stay here at least until you come, at the Emergency entrance."

He sat deep in thought, what would he do if Giuirdre didn't get better? What about if Giuirdre didn't get better? Or if she got better but not completely; could he look after her then? But then a woman came who was flustered, looking about.

"Joyce?" Sam asked.

"Yes; are you Sam?" What can you tell me about Giuirdre?"

"Well, it was lunch time, I had just been walking my dog as I do most days. We were gone about forty-five minutes, so Giuirdre wasn't there when we left; but when we got back, Jess, my dog, barked frantically at the back-garden gate; we ran up to the house, there we found Giuirdre, unconscious on the path. I ran in to get some blankets to make her comfortable and then called the ambulance. I went inside the house to get her address book and came here so I could call you. I don't know anything about her, in fact I have not seen anyone to ask, but then they wouldn't talk to me anyway, good job you're here now. That's all I know." His first tears began to flow. "I did all I could, I took her to the doctor and dentist, and the hairdresser, I was her neighbor, I was, I was,

and Nina too; were her friends and she was ours too."
Sam wiped his eyes, "Sorry, I have been sitting here wondering about her. With you here I might as well go and put her house to rights, maybe there could even be pots on the stove. All right, I'll bring you a key here tomorrow, I'll see you then; but, if there is anything, news or anything, please give me a call."
He took Jess with him and he made sure the house was closed up proper; he washed dishes and put them away, made Giuirdre's bed; walked around and put the furniture tidy and when there was no further work he reluctantly locked the front door and went back to his own boat.
The next morning, he went back to the hospital. There was no one there so he sat and waited and waited and waited; at last at lunch time Joyce came in. He went up to her and gave her the key, but his face had other questions. Joyce said that Giuirdre was very poorly and was going to be moved tomorrow.
"So, I can go and visit here there can't I?"
"No, I'm afraid not." Replied Joyce.
"Why not, why can't I go?"
"Giuirdre is being moved to a hospice."
"A hospice! That's where people go before they die. You can't send Giuirdre there."

"She is unconscious Sam, she isn't going to regain consciousness, her condition is slowly getting worse She will not get better."
His head slowly leaned forward, he leaned into his hands.
"Can I see her before she goes then?"
"Yes, I got the doctor to agree to that."
Together they walked into the bay. And there she was, much paler, much weaker, in bed with a pale blue robe.
Sam walked up to the bed, tears flowing down his cheeks, he stopped beside the bed, looking for something he couldn't see. He moved close to the bed and took one of Giuirdre's hands in two of his. He looked at her and said. "Goodbye Giuirdre, it has been a great pleasure knowing you.
Goodbye."
He and Jess wet home and they went for a long, long walk. Longer than ever before; Jess kept looking at Sam, making sure this was OK, Jess was uncertain about this walk. But part way in Sam knelt beside him and explained in considerable dog-detail what this long walk was all about; that they would never see Giuirdre again and there would be Jess, Sam and hopefully Nina and Tina.
So, the conversation on the river bank told Jess and Sam how things were going to be.

The next night Nina was to come was the night after next. Unless like on every other evening, Sam's thoughts about this one was sad.
When Nina came on the boat with Tina; she knew that something was upset.
"Sit down," said Sam, "times have changed. The first thing is that Jess found Giuirdre unconscious on the garden path; I got blankets and called the ambulance but now she is getting steadily worse and was moved to a hospice, I got to say goodbye, but that was all."
Nina was not surprised about the depth of Sam's demeanor, somehow, she knew that Giuirdre's fate was not all that caused the sadness that she could see.
"And - - - what else?"
Sam glanced at her with the love and pain he thought was coming.
"Nina, for many months I have loved you, even though the lives we have led together, with us and with Giuirdre, I asked you once what it was that kept you as far away as it did; you would not tell me what is was. Then I asked you if things might change; in a year, or in two years, you told me nothing would change. But now I have to know more; if you can't be more to me than you are now, I'm going away, if I could marry you or build some kind of life, that would change, but now I have to know."

Nina gathered Tina up, kissed Sam and told him that things could not change.
She made her way back on to the dock and Sam was all alone.

Chapter 2.—Follow your heart.

Follow your Saint, follow with accents sweet;
Haste you, sad notes, fall at her flying feet

Thomas Campion> *A Book of Airs.*

Sam told Arnold, his boss, thar he was going away for a while, he will call in when he got somewhere and pick up his work again. He had no address or phone number for Nina so his goodbye to her would be the one when she left that evening. He went to the boatyard and got the bottom of his boat painted, changed all the zincs and for his last stop at Giuirdre's pier to go and fetch a very large grocery shop-up, and then take his car to Arnold's barn for some period without end.

He had been coaxing Jess to do his business, without much success yet, on a large coir rug. He bent over him and told him the tale.

"Jess, we are going away, for a bit, for a while; I have looked at the weather and you and I are going offshore down to Cape May; you'll have to take some watches and you'll have to use the doormat – OK? I don't know what to do or where

to go, I only know you and I we have to make a change. So, Jess, off we go."
He started the engine and waited for it to warm up, he then shook off his doubts, undid the dock lines and turned the boat in a wide circle and headed out. Jess stood beside him for a long way and then he settled down in his bed. Sam stood out to sea, pointing at much southerly as he could but making best use of the wind. He kept a look at his thermometer, but it was early yet, at just after suppertime, with a sandwich and a cup of tea helping, he watched the temperature lower and he knew he was getting outside the Gulf Stream; he then turned as southerly as he could, still sailing well with the wind. He put the boat on auto-pilot and went below for two rugs more sandwiches, another flask of coffee, a scarf and gloves. He used one rug to cover Jess and got himself in position to be on helm all night.
In the morning all was well; the boat speed was still up,
"Been about 5.8 all night chortled Sam to Jess".
Sam got Jess's breakfast food and a drink of milk; Jess gobbled it all up and, reluctantly, made his way up to his bathroom, when finished he turned to face Sam. "OK, OK," said Sam, "I'll do it."
He took the rug and using the rope brail he attached to it, tied a short line and tossed it overboard to be towed and cleaned.

He engaged the auto-pilot then went below to wash his hands and fry two eggs, when done he sandwiched the eggs in two slices of bread and carried the on deck for his breakfast. The day went on, Sam edging the boat to westward the best he could. The next night was the same, Sam told Jess that the next day they could hope to turn north into the Delaware River. And so, it was the next day, Sam had to pick a time to go about and head north; he didn't know what would be best.
"Jess, I'm going to have a look at the tides, we need to ride the bay tide upstream so I had better take a careful look."
He went below for a few minutes and came up smiling.
"The tide is running out, and we are a couple of hours out so we can ride the tide up to the C&D canal and we can have a rest in Chesapeake City."
And so it was Sam was in good spirits so Jess was too, they made good time and saw the nuclear power station so Sam started the engine then hurried to lower the sails, a tanker passed them but it went on up the river, Sam and Jess turned left into the canal happily in easy reach of a place to anchor safely and have a rest. They could now see the bridge over the canal and as it grew closer they could see the restaurant and then Sam could see the entrance to the anchorage and they turned slowly in; quietly moving into the

anchorage Sam picked a place to anchor, they came to a halt and Sam lowered the anchor, measuring the rode; he stopped and just sat in the cockpit waiting for the boat to take up a position in the wind and the neighbors, satisfied he ruffled Jesses hair and said.
"OK Jess, we'll get the dinghy down and go for a run. He lowered the dinghy, got the harness and, put Jess in it on his chest and they climbed down the swim ladder into the dinghy, a few strokes of the oars and they were on the hard and Jess took off on an excited run on his own. Jess pulled up the dinghy and joined Jess for a long walk along the banks of the canal. They went back, Sam harnessed Jess and they were soon back on board. Jess got food and drink, when he was done with that, he joined Sam in the aft cabin for a long sleep.
Jess woke up first and was quiet for a while and then he stirred and Sam woke up as well. They had a snack for Jess and coffee for Sam and the he took them on another long walk along the banks of the canal up to a cemetery, and back the same way; Jess had a good run and now Sam wanted to make a good brunch of waffles, eggs, bacon (including a rasher for Jess) and fried bananas and fried bread. He ate it in the cockpit, it was quiet and still and rain seemed in the air; but Sam enjoyed his lunch, and pondering the rest of the

day, decided to have a glass of wine and then another lie down.
Rested and happy, the two of them set out the following day, motoring down the canal and into the Elk River and turning south. Sam thought he knew of a place to anchor; he had not been there but had heard about it from a friend. So, he sat in the cockpit and ruffled Jess's ears and told him not much further to go and maybe, he could have another run. He joined the Chesapeake Bay shipping channel buoys and followed down on the left side of the channel, he smiled and said.
"Jess, look at this place, it's called Still Pond Creek, look at it, and look at the depths, it's ten feet deep all over".
He motored off to the west side and anchored in the shelter of the land. He launched the dinghy and carried Jess over to the shore.
"Look Jess," he ruffled his ears, "look Jess, you can run all the way out there, far away and many, many things to investigate.
Sam settled the boat down and lowered the dinghy, with Jess in his truss they got settled in the dinghy and rowed to shore.
"There you are Jess, all that shore to explore, many things to see, all the flotsam to investigate for you, all clean from the water, you can look until you are content."

Together they walked the shoreline out to the bay, there were some places where Sam's boat shoes got wet and Jess's fur got wet and tangled, but they were happy, not yet quite as happy as they had been by Giuiudre's house, but more settled in their mands.

Back in the boat they sat in the cockpit and Sam brushed out Jess's coat and made him shine again. Then it was time for Jess's dinner and while he was eating it Sam poured a glass of wine. Jess finished off his dinner quickly, slapped his chops and came to sit with Sam.

"We'll stay here a couple of days", Sam said as he stroked Jess's back, 'I like it well, and I think you do too, see, he showed Jess his hand, sea glass that is, bits of glass been in the water a long time and made smooth like this, probably find more if I look carefully."

They went to bed early but arose early, They went for another walk and Jess did his business in the proper way, he ran unrestricted as Sam strolled along the water's edge looking for sea-glass; a work boat came out and made off out into the distance, at least Sam thought it was a work boat. Their stroll grew and took up most of the morning so Sam would be having a brunch and Jess a very late breakfast.

So, they stayed another day and then Sam had an idea.

"We'll stay one more day and we can have a surprise, you and me Jess."
The next day, in the late morning, Sam gathered up stuff in a large canvas bag, took Jess in his truss and left for the shore. Sam told Jess to go and play and he got together a ring of stones, a pile of dry driftwood, the meat grill from the stern grill and his treasures: two steaks, a fork, a bottle of red wine and two plates, knife and fork. He crumpled up some paper and spread small bits of dry wood and got a fire going, he built it up so there were some heavier bits and waited until the flames died down and then he called Jess.
"Jess, my fine companionable friend, you and I are going to share a barbeque, you and I, I shall have wine, but we both an have steak and bread. Now, but don't you tell anybody about this will you?"
So he put the grill over the rocks and placed the steak on the grill, the meat cooked quickly and when it was done he put one piece on a paper plate and cut it up, he laid it on the sand and motioned to Jess to eat it, Jess looked at him puzzled.
"Just this once Jess, we will have our meal together."
And they did. Jess consumed his with doggie gusto, but still unsure if it was all right or not.

Sam took more time with his wine, bread and biting pieces off the meat. But it was a companionable time, what Sam wanted.
Jess came and laid his head on Sam's leg and all was well that day.
They left the next day and made their way south, stopping at West River, Solomons, Fishing Bay, the Concrete ships and then on the Dismal Swamp canal and then to Elizabeth City where they had a free dock and walked to the grocery store for needed replenishments.
They went on, with Sam half-searching for destination, but still hurting that the life he had planned had fallen apart.
"We need to get some diesel," he told Sam, there is a marina coming soon and we can go in."
The pulled up at the gas dock, Sam pointed to Jess with a question mark.
"Sure, he can get out and stretch his legs."
Sam filled up with diesel and bought three gas cylinders for the pulpit grill.
"Do you know any waterfront places for sale that need fixing up?" Sam asked.
"No, nothing like that the man replied."
"What about that place up the river, the piers but nothing else." Said his helper.
"Oh, yes, been for sale when the owner died, his wife moved away but that's still here. It's about a

mile or so up the river, on the east side, you can go up and take a look."
Sam and Jess turned and headed slowly up river; and sure enough, there it was, Sam made his way over to look. The pier was new, the finger piers were new and well sized, the piers themselves were of new wood and the pilings were new and protected with plastic caps. He came up to the end of the pier and tied up. He and Jess went for a walk, along the pier and to the land. There was a small area of land close to the piers and it rose up a bank where there was a flat area. They walked up the path to see the flat area, it was sufficient to house a building and some other marina storage. Sam and Jess walked out the little roadway out to the highway, it was a part of a tiny village. They walked back out to the pier and called the phone number from the notice on one of the pilings.
"Forest real estate." The voice said.
"I have some interest in the pier down here on the river."
"Ah yes, the man who was working on that died; yes, it is for sale by his wife who moved away to live with her sister".
"Well, if it's for sale what is the asking price?"
"She wants $25,000."
"Oh," said Sam, "that's far too much for me. Sorry that I called."
"Well, do you want to make an offer?"

"No, I have cash to buy, I would like to talk to the planning office about it, but not at that price. But In fact, nothing like that price. Sorry."
"Can you tell me your number and perhaps I can make it work."
Sam gave his number and went back to the boat for lunch. The next day his phone rang.
"This is Jim Forest real estate; the owner would appreciate offers."
Sam thought, "What do you think that means?"
"I can't answer that, if you are interested have a chat with George Dwyer at the planning office, he'll tell you what has been approved and what might be approved. He will be in the office tomorrow."
Sam thought about it and then called for car rental to pick him up first thing tomorrow, but he asked when he made the request if well behaved dogs would be OK. The lady said OK but not as a driver. Sam hoped that it would be her who brought the car.
And, at 8:30, at was. Sam gave her a happy smile and he had a rug for Jess to lie on. They got directions and drove off to the planning office. Jess was told to guard the car and Sam went off to See Mr.Dwyer.
Mr.Dwyer was a nice man and showed Sam the plans of what had been approved. Sam thought

that was all right but there were things missing. He turned to Mr.Dwyer and said.
"If I give you a letter outlining the things I might add, if I bought it, would your office, or you, give me a letter saying if this was properly proposed it would get approved; a building, electricity for each slip, water for each slip, a septic system with a pump up from the slip level and well, those kind of things that I have not thought through completely."
"Not at all, I think from a planning office perspective that would be very good."
"OK, I'll go to the library and write a letter."
"Better than that; you can sit down and write it here."
Sam wrote an outline and left a copy with Mr.Dwyer. He drove of back to his boat and called Jim Forest.
"Any news?" He asked.
"Yes, she says she'll accept fifteen thousand from a cash buyer."
"Well, I'm a cash buyer. Do you want a deposit or can you gather up the paperwork for a land purchase and we do it all at once, I hope there will be a title search among all that."
Jim Forest said he could have the settlement ready in about a week. So, Sam asked for a car sales place ad drove there in the rental car. In a few days he and Jess went to Mike's Used Cars

and left with an older people mover. He had made a move and when the settlement was complete, he would have made a real move.
He asked “Mike of the cars”, Jim Forest and M. Dwyer about contractors. But he first followed Mr.Dwyer’s thoughts and went to visit Tom Long. He met him as he was adding some rooms to a small house so that a man and his wife could make a place for her mother.
“They needed a mother-in-law place but they don’t have much money, so I built this little apartment like a power boat, the kitchen is tiny and must be kept tidy, the living room has places for her best chairs and a nice site for her television; the bedroom has room for a single bed, a closet and chest of drawers and the bathroom has a hip bath to sit in or and a shower, the toilet has a lid that closes on its own. I think the apartment has everything that she wants, and anyway, she’s seen it and has made changes and helped me finish it. I must say I’m pleased with it. And anyway; you didn’t come to see this. Why have you come?”
“You’re a bit wrong, seeing your thoughts with this job has helped me. But I came to ask you about your work. Electric, water, septic system, industrial building with heat pump and insulation. That kind of stuff.”

"Well, there are some things I could get help with; the septic system and drain field, some electrical work and water might need approvals, but I could do all that."
"Come and have a look when you have a couple of hours. Give me a call, come for a visit on my boat, bring your wife if you have one." He gave Tom his number and he and Jess went home for an afternoon's rest.
In a couple of days' time he got a call from Tom about a visit.
"Do you know where to come?" Asked Sam.
"Oh yes, I know where to come, I thought I'd come in the afternoon and bring my wife. Will that be OK?"
"Yes, yes. I'll be looking for you."
About three-o-clock Jess raised his head and looked at Sam.
"Yes," said Sam, "they're a-coming along."
They both went out and Tom was walking down the dock with his wife and a little girl."
Sam went to meet them but first he knelt down and said to the girl.
"Hello, my name is Sam, and this is my dog, his name is Jess. If you hold out your hand he will come along and lick it, then you will be his friend and he will know you."
Tom's wife smiled and said.
"I'm Teresa, came with Tom to see your work."

She looked at her mother and then held out her hand, Jess came up and had a sniff, then he looked at her and sat beside her.
She looked at Sam but really talked to Jess.
"Hello, I'm Mia, I have come for a visit."
Jess looked happy and Sam stood up. He held his hand out.
Tom's wife smiled and said.
"I'm Teresa, came with Tom to see your work."
Sam waved his hand at the slips.
"All new, but the man who put them in died. I had a change in my life and I was looking for something to do. Jess ad I were sort of drifting along and we came upon this place. It has no value as it is, but I thought I would make it a marina for special people. I don't know what, but I want your help in getting it ready.
Now down here, on the docks, each slip has to have a water supply, a simple garden outlet with two connections, and each slip has to have a breaker box feeding two twenty-five ampere outlets. There must be a concrete sump to send the boat's sewage up to the septic system.
Now walking up to the bank of earth, I want a metal building up here, perhaps twenty-five feet long with good insulation and a heat pump, at one end there must be a room with the electrical system and with individual meters and a big

concrete sump will end here. I want a laundry room and a small bathroom in the building. Well, that's about what I want and for you to do it all. So, you can think about it and come back and tell me what to do, now you, Teresa and Mia come back to my boat for a visit."
They walked back along the docks, Sam helped Mia get on, Jess scrambled on in his usual way and Tom helped Teresa on. They went into the cabin and Sam got out some vanilla ice cream he said to Mia.
"If I knew you were coming I would have got special ice cream; tell me your favorite one and the next time you come I will welcome you with that."
"Ben and Jerry's chocolate chip."
"OK that's a promise."
The grown-ups sat back with a glass of wine and just talked about living there and what a nice place for children. Teresa blushed and said there was another on the way, the changes needed to their own house and when Tom was going to get on with them.
They left with some friendship between them and Sam looking forward to hearing Tom's proposal to do the work.
The work went well, the plan of the work, the planning office approval, the steady flow of

progress and Sam's progress payments took the burden from Tom.
At last the work was completed and Sam made the final payment to Tom. He asked them down to his boat one Saturday for brunch: smoked salmon on bagels, asparagus and a chocolate pudding for Mia; and Sam noted.
"There is Ben and Jerrys chocolate for desert".
He told Tom that he felt he was fortunate to have met him and got the work done under one boss. He knew how the payments would be folded by his accountants into the business, but to show his real appreciation he gave Tom and Teresa a thousand-dollar envelope, and one for Mia as well.
He wished them well and that he was looking forward to spending more time with Mia.

Chapter 3.—All is safely gathered in.

Safely, safely gathered in,
Far from sorrow, far from sin.
Henrietta Octavia De Lisle Dobree.
Children's Hymn Book.

Sam and Jess went about their business, but it was not much now; all the work was done and they were tidying up now; wondering where all this would lead- - or nothing. But then they heard the put-put-put of a sailboat engine, coming upstream; then they could see a boat with sails furled turning into their dock. They walked out to the end pier and waited, the boat came up and stopped; Sam took their lines and waited. Two women, in their fifties scrambled up on the seat lockers and said hello.
"I'm Olive and that is Pat; there are no other boats here, is it OK to be here?"
"Yes, I'm Sam and this is Jess, and you are welcome; we decided to make this a live-aboard marina, and you, well you're the first boat who's come here. If you want to stay pick a slip and I'll help you moor, stern in or bow in?"

So, Olive and Pat moved in and Sam told them to visit his boat in the late afternoon, wine or rum of tea or coffee he told them.
A bit later than four-o-clock Olive and Pat come for a visit; Jess lay quietly on the cockpit locker and watched. They came on board and sit themselves down, Sam offered refreshments and they all had white wine, except for Jess who had his solid food at this time.
"How long do you intend to stay." Asked Sam.
"We want to stay for a very long time; if you have us." Said Pat. "We want to point out what we are."
"Not bank robbers or spies." Laughed Sam.
"No," said Pat, "but other marinas have asked us to move so we want to get it done up front. You see, we were married to two brothers, for more than twenty years; we lived nearby and met often. Then Olive's husband got cancer, inoperable cancer and we all had to do what we could for him. He died and then my husband had a heart attack driving to work and he was gone too. Well, we didn't want two houses and I sold mine and moved in with Olive. We found that twenty years of being together had left its mark and well, we lived together, really together. That was all right until some local hooligans got together and made our life very unpleasant, so we sold that house and we had this idea that we could be boat

people, but, well that got unpleasant remarks at two marinas and we moved on until we heard about your marina and here we are."
Sam grunted. "This wine is really nice on a boat like this do'you know? Now tonight Jess and I put together a large onion pie that we can have with some new Irish loaf and some French bread. Do you want to join me? I have more wine, and by the way; First Rule at the Last Stop Marina is "Behave or Begone!" Now, come on, down below so we can talk when they pie is cooking."
Later they had cheese and crackers and chatted away and drank more wine while the pie baked. Sam said. "I don't know how to run a business, so when people come in, I shall ask them for a three month's deposit, to see if we like each other and after that a one year lease. The marina at the mouth of the river have a Travel lift so when you needed lifting, they can do it for you. What do you think of that?"
They thought it was OK but they still seemed a bit under the weather. And when the pie was done and they sat and Sam said.
"I used to have two friends; one day when Jess and I returned from a walk Jess barked and ran to the house where she lived; she was there unconscious on the path, I made her comfortable and phoned the ambulance. That was the last I saw of her until her daughter gave me permission

to say goodbye, she was still not conscious. My other friend Nina, used to come with her dog, a sister of Jess, and spend the night. I wanted to marry her, but, some reason would not let her. So, I left to make some mark somewhere, and here we are. Nobody says I'm a bad person living with my dog, and here, in my little kingdom, nobody says Olive and Pat are bad either; so, eat up and prepare to live here until you decide to move on."

Supper moved along and the girls and Sam and Jess had a very nice time. They talked of many things, but most among them was living together and living among other boaters."

Sam told them that their first experiences were odd and that other boaters would treat them as they are: borrow things, lend things, give a hand when is needed and be a neighbor and friend; you wait and see.

Olive and Pat went home to bed in a joint mood that they had not shared until the days when it became clear that they could live out their lives together.

The next day the girls washed and waxed their boat and took all their bedclothes to the laundry and Sam took his first ever money from the washer and drier. Their boat became a fresh air drier for all their stuff hung on the railings and some on the boom.

By mid-afternoon the boat was in Bristol condition and the girls, in freshly washed condition and hair finery came by and invited Sam and Jess for dinner. Later Sam and Jess reported for dinner bearing a bottle of wine as guests. Sam carried Jess down and he felt at home by finding a place beside their heating stove. Sam was interested in the boat as he would be in any boat, the boat was set up like any thirty-seven foot with the settees the well-equipped galley and the one large bed in the vee berth cabin. They had another conversation filled evening with good wine, the excellent pie made by Pat – but this time Olive said, we take it in turns to cook because the galley is small, next time it will have food from me!
Sam said that as, hopefully, the boats grew in quantity the dinners will be more in company with other owners, he didn't have one yet but he planned to have a garden barbeque arrangement for the boaters to have al fresco meals. Sam and Jess went home feeling that they had made the girls feel happier with their life style.
As Sam drew on towards his own boat he thought of how he would manage the boaters who came to live in the marina, he got on to his boat and he and Jess were together in the cockpit, Jess resting his head on Sam's knee, and Sam looking out over the river; thinking. He looked forward, hoping, that one day the marina might have enough

sailors that might make an eclectic mixture of peoples, outlooks, points of view and helpfulness that make a binding group that lived together. And he thought that if people came, who objected to Olive and Pat's lifestyle, then they will have to be moved on.

Chapter 4.

A man he was to all the country dear,
And passing rich with forty pounds a year.
Oliver Goldsmith The Deserted Village.

Olive and Pat were OK, they borrowed Sam's car and went off for a day foraging for food and other things they needed. Sam felt that they were happy with their lives together now.
About three weeks later another boat approached the docks and swung expertly into position, the pilot stepped off and made the boat fast before Sam got there.
Sam walked up and said.
"You know well about piloting your boat. Do you want to stay here for a while?"
"Well, yes, I heard at the marina upstream that you were planning to start a live-aboard marina. Is this true?"
"Yes, that's what I hope this is going to be. There is only one other boat besides me. Olive and Pat; that's their boat."
"OK, that's me, how do we get settled in here?"
"We begin with a ninety-day agreement, if we are both satisfied at the end of that then we have a one-year agreement."
"That sounds good to me."
"OK, which slip would you like?"

"A slip away from other boats. Not for me, you see I have my baby with me, don't want to cause distress with others."
"That's very nice, a baby on your boat, what a nice life you have to be sure, but don't you want to be by others? For company, for help, for any neighborliness, by Olive and Pat or by me. Anyway, come and meet Olive and Pat, see what you think. Don't worry about the baby, I'll go and get them, just a minute. Sam went and rousted out the girls and they came to meet her, excited as they could be about a baby.
They rushed up and said hello and said their names were Olive and Pat, what was hers?
"My name is Valery, call me Val, the baby is Francis, he is four months old."
Olive said. "Can't you be next to us, it would be fun to see Francis, maybe one day we could baby sit for you. We would be neighbors, that would be nice, we have never had a marina neighbor before, in fact, we have never had boat people who were very friendly at all. This place with Sam, well its very nice for us."
So that was that, Sam towed Val's boat back to the slip and Val tied it the way she wanted. Sam said to Val.
"Come by for a visit, later today when Francis is OK, make it a nice visit, have dinner with me and Jess."

In the evening Val came to Sam's dock and Sam pulled the boat in to make it safe for Val to step on with Francis.
"Come on below, Jess is there but he will just show interest in you both."
They went below and Jess did go up and had a sniff of Val, then he sat back and looked up at her, Val stood holding Francis and looking down at Jess; Sam said.
"I think he wants to say hello to Francis, he has not had a small friend like that before."
"Will he be all right?"
"I'm sure he will be."
So, Val gingerly lowered Francis down to Jess. Jess waited and when Francis was near enough, he stood up and walked over and sniffed Francis's face, then touched his cheek with a nose touch.
"There," said Sam, "now you will know Francis forever, and take care of him."
They made Francis a nest of cushions next to Val and Sam talked about the dinner for a bit later and asked Val if she wanted a glass of wine.
"Thought you might never ask."
As they had their wine Sam asked how it was that Val was there, piloting the boat, looking after Francis and now signing up for some period in a live-aboard marina.
"Like always, a string of circumstances. My mom died when I was fourteen and my dad decided to

press on; and we did, we spent most weekends on the boat, just me and my dad and he told me all about sailing. Then I 'spose as I got older and especially when I went to college, he wanted more adult company and he met a woman. In the end he married her. He gave me the boat and besides that there was some money left to me by my mother, not enough to live on, but, well enough to have. So, I qualified, got a job and then got in a pickle with a friend and finished up with Francis. The father hurried off and I had to decide my own fate. I could have terminated the baby, but, well, I think I wanted it. So here I am, in your place, wondering if I can make any money at some kind of job."
"So, what sort of work did you do?"
"Oh, I was a software designer."
"Well! Really, what sort of work did you do?"
"Mostly I worked on Internet catalogs, new ones, fix up old ones, make them work. My specialty, if you could call it that, was the stuff that customers call up and say it is hard to do: the connection of price, delivery cost, delivery times, all that stuff that make it happy or frustrating for the customer. But I liked the whole thing, but it was seldom that came along, but sometimes it did and then I could string it all together before I began."
"Do you have your lap top here with you?"

"Oh, yes, my whole life is here, me, Francis, work, everything I own is here."
'I am a software designer," said Sam, "have been for fourteen years; I worked for this guy when he was starting out, hung in there and here I am. I took a sort of leave of absence when my life began to fail apart, took a chance to buy this, it was only part finished, the previous owner died, the only thing was the pilings and the decks, everything else I added. So, when I decided to stay here, I went back to work again. If you have anything to show my boss, some completed work or something, I could ask if he could use you. If he does, I expect he would try for some small work that he could only check out a bit at a time. Anyway, it's up to you"
They had a nice evening and things broke up when Francis decided it was time for his supper.
The next day Val sent some email of her work for Sam to send to Armond. He got an email back almost by return asking for Val's address and so Val got a live-aboard slip, an Internet connection, new neighbors, a job and some peace she wasn't sure existed anymore.
Sam looked after her for a little while; they took Francis and went shopping for a car seat for him; then went to the grocery shop, and the wine shop and a tour of the village shops and then for coffee. With Francis settled in his new seat they took him

into a coffee shop for a rest before going back home.

"You're very nice about settling us in," said Val, "we feel very settled and peaceful."

"You seem young to be alone like you are," said Sam, "you be sure to let me know if you need anything, and, well, don't be all alone, Olive and Pat are anxious to be a help, really anxious, don't let them be out there looking in, do let them help."

But, with a job with Arnold Val seemed content on her own.

Chapter 5.

But who hath seen the Grocer
Treat housemaids to his teas
Or crack a bottle of fish-sauce
Or stand a man a cheese
Earl of Chesterfield. *Song Against Grocers.*

It seems this marina 'where ever it was that advertised Sam's live-aboard place' did a good job, it was in another few weeks and another boat approached, but with the helmsman waving arms for some help.
Sam ran down and a woman shouted for help with her husband. He tied up their boat and rushed aboard to help; the husband was lying on the cockpit locker writhing in something that made his arms tight across his chest and for him to call out in language that Sam could not understand.
"We must get him to the doctor." Said Sam. "Wait here and I'll get some help."
He went to fetch Olive and Pat and together, with the wife, they hustled the sick man up the dock and into Sam's car. Sam drove with the wife looking after the man to the Health Center in the village. Sam went in leaving the wife with the man. Sam found a doctor who told them to bring him in. They lay him on an inspection couch, Sam went outside and waited in the waiting area. After

about an hour the wife guided the man out, he seemed quiet and normal to Sam. They went out and Sam put them in the car, but then he went back in to the doctor. He looked at the doctor. The doctor said the man had become overwrought, with all the trials and tribulations leading up to their latest life. He said he had given the man a shot and two tablets his wife could give him; but he said the man was OK and wouldn't be a problem and take him on home and if he had a good sleep then he would be well.

Sam drove home and helped the wife take the man to the boat, he helped them into and made to leave, the wife offered the seat and said she would get her husband in bed and come and talk to him.

She did come back and offered coffee and home-made cakes. She asked about staying there and Sam told her the usual tale about the ninety days provision; she smiled at that and said that suited them very much. She told him that long ago they were from Belarus. Her name was Olga and her husband's name is Matvei; but they had to leave where they lived because of a caucus real estate claim, between family factions; they had to move; they were Jewish and were afraid that some fate would befall them. They moved across the borders to Poland, but they couldn't find a place to call home and they joined a group of homeless people being looked after by some charity. Eventually they came to the United States and began a new life. They both got jobs and eventually saved up enough to buy a small store front in the outskirts of Newark. Here they began a small home grocery store; they get it going, got sources for food, drinks and all that stuff; but they found out that, yet again, the people around them were against them.

"The whites, the colored and most others; but it was the colored that were the main trouble, to Matvei, they would come in the store, maybe six of them and two would be a problem for Matvei and the rest would shoplift all over the store. They stole more than we could make. So, we again sold the store and decided to try the boat, nobody else to worry about. But Matvei's memories grew and grew until, well, you saw him today. Now I don't know what to do."

Sam said. "Don't do anything, don't plan or worry; you both settle in here, all the people here are friendly and helpful; you don't know what will come, just let Matvei settle down, have a rest; and in a couple of days come for dinner on my boat.

Sam left it like that for the time being.

Two days later Sam stopped by and asked after Matvei; he is OK said Olga, he said we should invite you for dinner, so what about tomorrow?

At about six he went with Jess to their boat and banged on the cabin and Olga looked at and invited them in, Jess got a big beef bone in the cockpit and Sam went below.
"You feeling OK now Mavei?"
"Yes," he smiled, "very well; and thank you for helping me; I'm afraid I got into a stylish? Is that how you say that, stylish?'
"Well perhaps you mean latest or something, anyway, we know how you felt and how to deal with it, so don't think about it, think about being here, being happy, no one to bother you or cause trouble, you are all right here. I promise you."
Olga brought beer for the men and they talked while she was finishing dinner.
"You had trouble, leaving Belarus and finding your way here?"
"Yes, we did," answered Mavei, "in Belarus we got involved in a family fight, over some land, well quite a lot of land. We supported Olga's parents, but things got very difficult, very emotional and vicious; it was better if we left, it made peace again, well, not peace, but without conflict. So here we are, Mavei wants to have a grocery store, that's what he wanted, he was happy at first in Newark, but when we finished the store and opened it things began to get worse and worse, so again we had to sell up and move on.

Sam had dinner with them and went away with some ideas of helping them.
In a couple of days Sam went back to talk to them. Look you two, I thought about your story; here is a silly idea. Why don't you think about opening a store, here, here in the marina. We have the building, it is airconditioned and would be a good place for a small store; there are not many boats in here, but that will change. Meanwhile we can plan. Now one thing that would work very well, and you can start it now; is to be a delivery for groceries, you can make an arrangement with a local store and the boat people can give you a list and you can get them their groceries. You can charge extra for the delivery, but when all more than twenty slips are occupied you will have a big order to get, once or twice a week. And we can start a small store in the building, with proper storage and you Olga can be in charge of that part. If we start this now and boaters get used to it, then the new boats will fall in line. If you agree; I'll buy a van to get the groceries in and we can buy some used storage and furniture for the shop. Well, anyway, think about it and let me know.

Chapter 6.

Shades of the prison-house begin to close
Upon the growing boy
William Wordsworth *Ode, Intimations of Immortality.*

Less than two weeks after Olga and Matei came two trawlers appeared of the marina. Sam went out to greet them and to ask if they were coming to stay or move on. They both said they wanted to stay so Sam told them to tie up at the end of the docks. One of them had to face the other way to get their pump out vent close to the dock, the other was OK.

Both were crewed by newly retired couples. Sam had begun to think he might have to get another courtesy car to handle all the traffic, but then, as he began to think that, a new idea began to grow in his mind. He would explore that later.

They were trawler-people, not like the sail boat ones. The trawler people had nice Sperry Topsiders all clean, white socks khaki pants and nice tops; but they were very friendly and wanted to know about the other slip owners and the rules for renting. Sam told them about his ninety day and then one year, they all nodded when they heard that and smiled.

Frank and Winnifred were one couple and Gavin and Jen the other; Jean said they always had a happy hour about four so he was invited today, he asked if Jess was OK and she said he was so Sam went off to find a good pair of pants and general tidy-up.

He came by about four with Jess and his carry-dog carrier, Sam climbed up on the

Aft deck and put Jess down for him to meet the people; satisfied Jess lay down beside Sam and drifted off to sleep. Sam told them how the marina came to be and he told them of his plan to stay here a long time.

Frank and Gavin looked at each other and nodded, "OK", so Frank said they wanted Sam to come for a drink but, there was something else they wanted to tell him.

"Well", he said, scratching his head, "well you see we are hoping, well expecting, some police officer to come by and take us in. We got ourselves in a bit of a bind, you see, Gavin and I worked for this sort of entrepreneur, at least that was how we thought of him; I looked after the trucking part of the business and Gavin looked after the properties; we had worked there for fifteen years and we were both happy. But about a year ago small things began to change; truck mileages sometimes were not what the trip called for, much more, a great deal more. When I announced this to our boss, he didn't show any interest, and then in Gavin's world buildings and houses appeared in the records without Gavin having known about it. Then we overheard from some pub conversations about all the girls seen with our boss, but he was happily married, or so we thought. But this girl rumor seemed to persist, but not the same girls. We didn't know what to do; our boss would not welcome any of our involvements in an activity that he wanted kept secret, so we did nothing. But then two things happened: the first was his personal safe was left open in the wall, well, it had six hundred thousand dollars in it. The door was open and inside on one wall was a label with the safe door deposit written on it, so we recorded the number, shut the door and went on about our business. The second thing was late one evening we were on our way home from a skittles match and we saw six or eight girls get out from one of our trucks and into a people carrier driven by someone we didn't know. Gavin and I talked about this and we concluded that he was trafficking people, well, mostly girls. We thought about it and decided to advance our retirement a bit. We sold our houses and we bought these two homes, and we really call them homes, these are our future homes. But at work then we didn't know what to do, this business, if that was what it was, is very bad, bad for the girls and what future there will be for them; in the best circumstances they could be domestic helpers, but they didn't look like that, and what was it that produced that pile of money. So, we decided to show him a way to stop. So, we took the money from his safe and put it in a safe deposit box in a bank close to where we worked. We thought it would make him come to us and we would say he could have t provided the traffic stopped. Well, that was four months ago, but nothing has happened, we thought he would get the police to come for us. So; we are waiting for the police to come."

Sam grinned.

"What another nice thing you got me too Ollie. So, what do you want to do?"

"Well, wait for the police to come for us, and then we can tell them all we know."

"But you don't know anything, and you are thieves."

"Yes, I know; that's what's bothering us."

"So where did this all take place."

"Oakham."

"Well, that's not far away, tell me the name of the pub there and Jess and I deserve a day off anyway, we'll go and sniff around. So, that's that and how about another glass of wine."

Next day Sam called the Pub, “the Ship” and asked if they could rent a room for a couple of nights, but he had a well-behaved dog.”
They told him a twenty-dollar dog deposit to be returned if all was well. Sam said he would be there soon after lunch. And so, they had some time all to themselves.
It was less than an hour and they were both settled in the bar with a pint, well, at least Sam was. When he got his drink, he asked the barman about the company called Marston’s, he said he had been told he might get a job there.
“It’s about two miles up that road, but I don’t know about a job there, the owner’s been arrested and is in jail pending trial, I don’t know what is happening up there.”
He drank his drink and drove off in the direction of the place; he found it and parked outside wondering what to do. Eventually he went inside and asked someone he met about a job.
“Don’t know about that, Mr. Marston has been arrested and we don’t know what’s happening. Best you go and see Mrs. Marston and see what she thinks. She’s at their nice place down the road about a mile.”
So off they went, wondering still if this was a good thing to do.
They pulled in at “the nice house” and rang the bell. A woman came to the door looking

expectantly for something, she had a look of wanting something, needing something. Sam thought about his "getting a job ploy" but then, on the spot, decided a more involved approach would serve better.

"Mrs. Marston, I recently met people who knew about your husband's troubles, now I have no power or anything, but I wonder if I can help in any way?"

The woman stared at him, and paused, then, "Come in come in, and your dog, come on in."

Sam sat down and looked at her.

"I know your husband has been arrested, but is he in a position to be helped?"

"No, not at the moment. A few days before he was arrested a thief took a great deal of money from his wall safe, so he can't yet afford bail. He's in there because of something he did for me," she smiled, "I am from Poland. For a long time I have been trying to make a way for young girls to come here and make a new life.

It's very difficult. So, with my sister in Poland I hatched a plan; bring the girls here and provide a place to stay and to work. When they earned enough, they could buy fake. Documents and begin a new life. My husband converted an old building to have lots of tiny apartments and there the girls stayed. It was illegal, but, not to me anyway, very harmful. The girls mostly became domestic helpers under my sort of sponsorship some found better jobs; all working for their future. Then local gossip caught up with us and the legal girls stayed in their apartments but the illegal ones went elsewhere. And that was when the police came, arrested him for rumors."

"Who is running the company now?"

"Nobody really, the two men who did run it retired, I'm afraid we didn't appreciate all they did, but, well, regrets that's all they are."

Sam paused and then spoke up.

"Mrs. Marston I'm going away to see what I can do to help. Would you give me your personal phone and I will call you very soon with some improvements?"

He left with Jess and told the pub he had been called away.

He got back to the marina and went to his boat for lunch for him and Jess. When they had settled down and gone for a dog-walk they got Jess's carrier and went back to the trawlers. Sam climbed up and settled down, he looked at them all, he smiled.

"You lot are the worst detectives in the world. "The girls" as you call them were illegally imported by Mrs. Marston in concert with her sister in Poland, to give them a chance for a better life. The "mysterious building" you thought of was a building converted to tiny flats for the girls to live in while they earned enough money to buy fake papers, some were domestics in places found by Mrs. Marston, some were better qualified and got better jobs. Mr. Marston is in jail because he doesn't have enough money for bail, nor for a good lawyer. The business is in bad shape because the two men who made it run well had retired, but would be welcomed back at improved working conditions.

Here is Mrs. Marston's personal number. I think she would be glad to hear from you, especially if you suggested places you could look for the lost money. And, you could live here and drive in there every day, and Winifred and Jen can become involved here with the picturesque people here. And no police will come."

Chapter 7.—The Repairman.

A man Sir, should keep his friendship in constant repair.
Samuel Johnson. *Lord Chesterfield's Letters*

Soon after the trawlers came an oddity, even for a marina. Sam got up with Jess for their first morning walk and there, tied up aft of one of the trawlers was another sail boat. Still, he and Jess went about their morning walk, make sure all the boats were OK, walk out towards the road and see if there were animals to see and for Jess to do her business. When he got back there was a person sitting in the dock with a cup of coffee, Sam walked up and said. "Hello."
"I am the Repairman." Said the new man. "Do you want to come for coffee?"
"Yes, that would be nice. Can Jess come too?"
"Well, yes; but Jess might have a bit of a shock. I have a ferret. His name is Hobo, he's very friendly with most other animals, but first encounter might be a bit of a meeting. But no harm will come I'm sure."
Sam got on the boat and Jess followed him; Sam sat on the locker, took his cup of coffee and put his arm around Jess. Jess already was aware that something was not normal and his nerves were sprung, ready for something, something not yet

understood. The new man sat with his coat fastened about him as he sipped his coffee, but then, at the side of his neck and little foggy face looked out.

Jess stared at the little face, then at Sam, confused. Then the face disappeared, Jess relaxed; then the little foggy face looked out from the wrist of the coat. Jess was more perplexed, “two of ‘em?” But no, the face went back inside; then out again at the neck. Jess kindled up against Sam and Sam rubbed his head and leaned over and said. “That’s Hobo, the ferret, he could be a friend of yours if you’d like him.”

The man, Dave was his name, took Hobo out of his coat. “There’s a big breast pocket in my coat, he likes it in there, warm and protected. He held him in his hands. Hobo was still and at peace.” Dave held him and offered Sam the chance for Jess to say hello. Sam leaned over to Jess and whispered. “Do you want to say hello to Hobo?” The two animals were tempted but not ready for full freedom of each other. Sam put Jess on the cockpit sole to make his mind up. Dave let Hobo out of his grip to find his place. Then, all of a sudden there was playing and chasing, with Hobo doing his sensuous cornering and Jess reaching for Hobo without touching. Dave and Sam sat there for about ten minutes without any desire to interfere, in the end it was ended by animal mutual consent over time spent in constant conflict and peace came.

"Well do you want to stay here?" Asked Sam.

"I will if you say you want me," said Dave, but you better know a bit more about me, come on down below."

They went below and it was like most boats, settees, cook stove, refrigerators, cooking tool, pilot berth; all the usual boat stuff.

"Then," said Dave, "come and look forward, "he opened the vee berth door and there was a miniature machine shop in there."

Sam looked at it.

"A three and a half inch lathe, a small milling machine, a drill press and racks and racks of hand tools. Why, why wouldn't any marina want to have you in their ranks?"

"Some of 'em are afraid of me taking away some of their work."

"Well, you're welcome here my man, very welcome, choose your slip and make yourself at home."

Dave made himself at home in the slip most closer to the water on the upstream side of the dock. He settled in with Hobo who caused great mirth with the other slip holders.

The Repairman, as Sam called him, began his career with a job for Val; she wanted to be able to run a heating stove from the propane container on her boat. Dave took a look at it and told her it would require a separate line from the container to the stove.

"The stove requires full strength propane from the bottle. It's quite safe but it will require a manual shut off valve in your propane locker and a twelve-volt solenoid in the boat. I can order the parts for you, and it will be quite safe for you and Francis. So, he did that and then he got onto Sam to get a little propane refill-station for someone to refill all the propane on the boats.

"Be a useful thing to have in a marina."

So, Dave got the propane station to look after as well.

Before long Dave was busy with jobs for many of the boats; because he was able to turn, mill, cut threads, and work in marine materials the boat owners were able to have devices and accessories that they only dreamt about before.

Another boat-liver found a place to be and earn enough money to get along.

Chapter 8.—Boat of Long-Ago

But still the hands of mem'ry weave
The blissful dreams of long ago
George Cooper. Sweet Genevieve.

Things were not ordinary, not in this marina. A new sail appeared: gaff-rigged, very long boom shining in the late afternoon sunshine; it seemed a vision from long ago when Sam saw it; dark green hull with varnished mast and boom, the boat cutting upstream in the diminishing western breeze. Sam stood there and watched it as it slid away from them, hoping it would come in for a visit on his way back down stream. But then it turned, into the wind and then on facing down-stream; it turned with the wind at her stern and then later again it turned back towards the marina, the boat turned into the wind and slowed, the helmsman went forward and the jib slid down and was fastened; then the boat turned towards the marina, with just enough way to be maneuverable; when he got to the open dock where Dave had originally tied up, the helmsman cast off the mainsheets and grasped the dock with a very long pole. Sam was there by this time and pulled gently on the pole and the boat was docked.

“Thank you,” said the helmsman, “a very grizzled young-looking man who was accompanied by a spritely middle-aged greyhound. “Thank you, these days deck hands are young men with not much else to do but wear fancy dock clothes. Are you the marina that boasts very live-aboard slip holders?”

“Yes, that’s us, we all live aboard boat people.”

“Any room then?”

“For you? The very best.”

“At last, a place to relax and be an ordinary boat person.”

“Well, you can do your own thing, but the people here with not let you do it alone. You can get all tidied up and come and visit me on that Morgan, but on your way to me there will be several people who will offer you dinner or a beer or something. Oh, and bring your friend with you when you come.”

In a couple of hours, they came. He told Sam his name was Arthur and his dog’s name was Duke – not because I called him that, you understand, but that was his name when he raced. I didn’t know him then; we met when we needed each other, I needed a friend and Duke had urgent need of a home. We have been together ever since, five years, and good years they have been too. He had a place on the conveyer to the abattoir, I had need of a friend. All I had was this old boat;

originally built for my grandfather and passed on to my father; and then to me; but sadly, it was nearer to firewood than a boat then. I got a job and I found some retired boat carpenter and together the hull was restored until it could float. Then Duke and I lived on it, finishing the work at we went. My carpenter made the mast and the boom and the jib boom and we made it habitable over time, settees, bed, cookstove, heater all working now. But we are a bit tired and are looking for something where my employee pension and Social Security pays the rent and perhaps some other work besides.

"Would you and Duke care to join me and Jess for a coffee, bottle of beer or a glass of wine?"

"That will be welcome, not many boat people have been that way. Will Duke be a problem do you think?"

"No, He'll be all right, Jess can be company for him."

They walked up to Sam's boat and got settled, in one on each settee and Duke and Jess dozing together by their feet.

"Is your boat OK? Are you all settled in? Water, electricity? We have a portable device to empty your holding tank; then you can empty it in the sump, wash it with water and the pump will send it up to the holding tank. And we have a courtesy car you can use to go shopping when you have to.

So, what do you have: coffee, tea, beer or join me in wine; today it is just a red table wine"
"A glass of wine would be fine for me."
They talked for a few hours; mostly Sam asking how Arthur handled the maintenance of the one hundred and ten-year old hull.
"Not difficult, now we have it up together. I haul it every year and do whatever repairs are evident; but the work we did before is holding up well, we have to pay attention to along the water line but she still is good. She is a very good boat for us; the decks and the house top are all painted canvas so they are waterproof, we pay attention to the cockpit, the seat lockers are covered too, but there are areas that are wood, so we look to those pretty often. Below she is very nice, we have modern refrigeration and stoves when it is cold; two stoves actually, a propane stove to keep us warm and a wood or coal stove when we want to feel blessed, but bringing coal and wood in, if you can have time enough, and taking it out again makes it a thing we use occasionally, it was installed when the boat was built so we wouldn't want to remove it."
They enjoyed each other's company so Sam suggested Arthur stay for dinner before he went home again. The dinner drew into an evening's entertainment mostly of Sam listening to Arthur's tales of adventures and harassment in his boat

and some liqueur after dinner. Finally, they found some bowls and fed Sam and Duke and went off for a walk together before bedtime. They parted and Sam walked home but then asked Jess if he would like another walk. They went back their way, Jess involved in doggie stuff and Sam beginning to ponder over his life at the marina. He had achieved what had been in his mind at the beginning; but here has was now, with all these sailing friends, his remote work for Arnold was going well, no, well, but no Giuirdre to visit, no pride in doing something for her; and even more, no Nina or Tina to come to stay, he even thought, well, sometimes, that the way their relationship was ended was too sudden; too sad; and much of it to him. Still there they were, Sam and Jess, sailboat people normal; that's what they were. Sam heaved a sigh and they turned back to their boat.

Chapter 9.

Three hours a day will produce as much as a man ought to write.
Anthony Trollope. Autobiography

Toward the end of the summer days the last boat came to pass. Sam and Jess were sitting on the dock, Jess with his head close to Sam's leg, Sam dangling his feet in the water. They watched the boat as the sails were lowered and a puff of smoke as the engine was started.

The boat edged closer and the fore deck person asked if this was the live-aboard marina where long term sailors were welcome.

Sam said they were welcome and they were the last boat he could welcome.

The sailor asked how long they could stay.

Sam said if they stayed a probationary period of ninety days then they would be a one-year lease after that. The man said OK and asked where their slip would be; Sam waved them in and helped them tie up.

"My name is Godfrey, this is Phillipa, God and Phill."

"My name is Sam, this is Jess, we run the marina, but there is not much to run. There is electricity, I bill you based on what the company bills me, there is water, I don't know about the winter yet for water; we have a portable tank for draining holding tanks, there is a place to empty it and wash it so the sump pump empties it. There is a courtesy car for you to use, and, that about it, besides the people here will be interested in you."

"Well,' said Phill, "we are here because we both write, I write because I'm hoping it will be a part of my DiPhil but God is writing a novel. We won't get in the way of others, and we just want to be a part of a little community."

"We want you to be a part of the community," said Sam, "we are an integrated sort of sailing community and lots of help is available if you want it. Why don't you come to the Morgan over there for cocktails about five?"

At four Jess gave a chuckle-bark and God and Phil came on board, bearing a bottle of wine. Sam had made a leak pie and a quiche Lorraine with bread from Matzie's store and three guacamoles; they settled down with their wine and God and Phil seemed happy to be there, Phil kept stroking Jess's head with his toes, to Jesses great satisfaction as he moved closer for better coverage. Sam told about the marina, how he discovered it and the great contact he made with Tom to get all the work done; he outlined the 'characters' living thee and the peaceful existence they seemed to enjoy, the grocery store and the grocery deliveries, if they needed any, the propane store run by the Repairman and any other help they need.

Sam asked them about their writing, God said.

"Well, they were both deep into their work but the life they used to live got in the way of work; so owning their boat, they decided on a break to see if their writing would rise to what they thought of it, or, move on to other things, they were going to work and try hard to see if, well one of them will do well.

Sam said to God.

"You said your work was for a DiPhil, what can you write all out here in the woods?"

"I did an economics degree, I didn't choose that, my father did, but that's what I did' it didn't satisfy me on I went on to do a Master's but that left me cold as well, I could not see me doing much work in the world with that. So, I tried for a doctorate program with a professor that I had read about, but I never thought would take me; but he did; so here I am. My dissertation is on the one economics conundrum that has much interest to me, it puzzles me and I don't know how to write about it, but I am."

"What is that?" Asked Sam as he poured another glass of wine.

I have always thought that decline in original thought has an influence on economy but that is not thought of at all; you see, the industrial revolution in the western countries, grew from rich people getting richer from the efforts of others, not so rich; in fact a replica stemming from the enclosure age in England, and similar land-grab events in other places, there is no way to ignore those. What interests me is the underlying roots of intelligence and original thought in a group of people outside of this.

Take the last two hundred years, think of changes; in France in about 1800, after the Revolution, a new art Neoclassicism grew up, women painters were at least noticed, painters like Delacroix and Corot produce work that is highly valued today; a hundred years later, those paintings were painted by Degas, Manet, Gauguin, Monet and lots of others, Picasso came and swept the board, writers gathered in Paris and wrote, performers like Josephine Baker was an icon and went on to be a resistance heroin. When the war was over peace came slowly in Europe, but there were groups of people, engineers for example, that did wonderful things with motor cars, thing that are in use today. But along came WWII and things changed again, After the war there were eight companies manufacturing commercial aircraft in the US, now there is only one. In all the world countries have changed to “the world economy” but it seems to me that the mind-set, and the world economy, have been the demise of individual thought. Of course, all this has been involved in "the digital age"'. Here, anything on the web is true, any advertising is true, anything true is false, we are slaves to the system where without the net you are trapped - - - or free.

My dissertation hopes to sort this out – quantify it. But it is hard to stuff it all into words."

Sam said.

"My thoughts are just like yours; this boatyard is full of the people you want to write about, you should have long conversations with them, they will each be able to give you some history that will help you think. Sam turned to Phil, can you tell about your work?'"

"Well yes, but it is just a story I invented, based, a little in parts, from some friends and their experiences, I set out with much of my story written in my head, but now I have come to a halt; there is nothing more to write, not yet."

"Are you happy with what you wrote?"

"I suppose so, but being stopped makes it hard. My story centers around a young girl, eighteen or a bit more; she was a tennis player, and a good one too; Her father was her driving force, he rented time with big coaches and he got her to play in tournaments of increasing competitiveness, but she increasingly did not like her life. She played in a tournament, and won, she was on the court and waved to her father and then turned back to the dressing room, there was a news stand there carrying a camera, as she went by it collapsed, mostly on her and primarily on her legs. After exhaustive tests it was decided to remove, below the knee, the left leg. The surgeon was examining her when her father visited, “no more tennis for you,” he said. She smiled at the surgeon and said, “I shan’t be troubled with him anymore,” and she never did. But she was alert; she found lists of lawyers and found a young lady lawyer. She called her in and told her she would be her lawyer in getting compensation for her loss. She was instructed that she was the only person able to speak for her and she was empowered to act for her in this matter, and only her. This notice was just in time to cut off her father’s efforts to get the insurance to talk to him. She stayed with her lawyer while things were in motion, she went around looking for a place to build a tiny house away from people, she found a ten-acre field near the farmhouse and she bought that. To go on quickly, she had a very small house built with a small barn, she got a pond dug and a well-driller made wells for her house and to control the pond. She got a large dog she called Dennis and ram called Kellie and a dam called Nellie. She had two of her acres fenced with electric fence and got Jersey cow that she learned how to milk. She swam in her pool and slept out

some nights. She used the milk from her cow and what was left went on to curdle and she made cheese and butter. She had all this in order, she spun yarn from sheep's wool she saved, Dennis was a friend; all was good; except she felt there was something missing but she couldn't decide what it was.
And that's where my story stands now."
If you poke around here and talk to the people; I'm sure some thoughts and ideas may come."
They stayed until the darkness ad long since settled there and then went home together, but Sam was on his own.

Chapter 10.

What is better than wisdom? Womman, And what is
Better than a good womman? No-thing.
Geoffrey Chaucer The tale of Melibeus.

Sam was wrong when he told God and Phill that they were the last ones of the season, a month later, on a day of gusty rain showers, a bit by luck of walking back from the car, he saw a boat cruising in, he walked out to the dock and welcomed the sailor, in foal weather suit and a watch cap as she was tying up to the dock.
"Is this the live-aboard marina?" Was the first question.
"Well, it is; and we were closed for several weeks. Have you come far?"
"From Long Island, I had a slip there but the house was sold and I was asked to move on. I came south looking for a place like this, but it seems there are none. But you have no slips to rent me?"
"No, I do have a slip and you can have it; it is next door to a lovely wooden boat and a middle-aged Greyhound called Duke, it was just that we were feeling kind of full when the last one came in. No, you can move down that lane; and I'll be there to help you tied up."
Sam got her safely in and then asked.

"Are you alone?"
"Yes, all alone. My name is Nancy, Nancy Holden."
"Well, you can find friends here, but if you prefer not to, well that's all right as well. He told her about the water, electric and the sewage and issued an invitation to visit his boat for wine before dinner and smiled at her."
She did come to dinner, with her foul weather clothes changed for something, well, not for visiting, but OK for an impromptu visit for wine and chat.
He had a Giuirdre's cheese and egg pie he had made and a bottle of white wine.
"Here you are, glass of wine and egg pie for food, then you can tell me all the tales of your ejection and trip down."
"My boat belonged to my cousin and her husband, I used to sail with them all the summer; he became too poorly to sail the boat and then my cousin sailed it on some weekends. Then, I didn't know if she wanted to not sail any more, or if her husband got jealous, well, I think it was that. Anyway, they gave me the boat and I was able to keep it at the dock of her friend's house. I was working and that was good. Then the house got sold and I had to move. I went to a marina but nothing seemed the same; then things got bad at work and that did it for me. I got rid of everything and headed south, not at great speed however, it

has been two years since then, I have languished in four or five places but never yet found somewhere to settle down again; so here I am trying your home here."

"You are welcome; standard practice is for a four-month lease and if we like each other and then a twelve month lease, there is a list of boat owners that I like a lot here, all kinds of different people, different backgrounds, even a young single mother with a small child. But all kinds of people. I bought this place unfinished by the man who started it, just the pilings and dock. So, I had it finished, it was something of a risk for me, at that time, no slip people, no prospects, but here we are less than a year later with people who say they want to live on board.

I'm a bit like you, my boat was at a house and I was happy being a tenant of the house owner, she was a good friend to me, but she died and another friendship failed so me and Jess came south like you did and finiished up here, made it a good marina for 'live-aboards' and here we are.

"We are in a small village here, but there is a courtesy car here to use, but if you want to go out to work, you'll have to buy a car."

"No, no, I have enough to live on and pay your fees, I have some shares left from when I worked for an insurance company, he sold out but somehow my name was left out of the list of

shareholders and I got to keep mine, they are not very exiting but they do provide some income, and I have to money invested from the sale of my house so, providing I am careful, I shall be OK. You said I'm next door to a middle-aged Greyhound called Duke?"
"Ah yes, well he belongs to Arthur. Arthur's grandfather had his boat built, then his father had it, but by the time Arthur got it, it was falling down, he got a job and found a retired carpenter to help him and slowly they got the boat hull all in good shape; then Arthur lived on it, he has all mod-cons and even has the cast iron wood and coal stove put in when the boat was new, but he has more modern heating for most times. Then he needed someone or something to add in his life, and he met Duke, that was his racing name, he was on a conveyor that eventually would take him to euthanasia, so they joined forces and eventually got here, so he's another sailor who has found a home."
So, Grace sat and talked with him and rubbed Jess's ears, they had a one for the road and she went home.

Chapter 11—The Grocer.

But who hath see the Grocer
Treat housemaids to his teas
Or crack a bottle of fish-sauce
Or stand a man a cheese?
Gilbert Keith Chesterton   Song Against Grocers.

Sam had always thought of making the marina, making it more of a village, more self-centered, but not so much self-centered but self-governing, but not that, he wanted his people to be happy and stay happy.

This was his first attempt at that. He visited Val who was good with computer pages and lists and asked if she could construct a list for a tablet. But a list that had say thirty pages to fill in and there can be several pages for each set and that it could keep the set and keep each set of pages for three times. She said that would be easy for her and Sam said he would be back.

Then he went to Olga and Matvei. He banged on the boat and asked if he could talk to them. In fact, he asked then to walk with him and Jess up to the laundry.

When they get there, he told them.

"When I built this building there wasn't much of a plan; I wanted a place for the electrical circuit breakers and I wanted somewhere to locate the

washers and driers. I wanted two personal toilets and showers but that was all that was planned. This long," and he waved his arm over the empty part of the building, "was for something I did not know of then. But now I think I know what it is. See, I want you to see, I think there needs to be a cooled display case here, perhaps two, and a refrigerated display case here, there could be fresh food display cases of vegetables etc. here. Now, but what makes this is going to work is that that you will have a special tablet display to write lists in. But every week you visit each boat in the marina and write down there shopping list, the boat signs it and off you go to fetch it and bring it home and get paid. Maybe three mornings a week you go and do that. I will buy a second hand van for you to use. When you are off doing your rounds Olga can run the store here. So, if you are careful you could have household supply for all of our slips.
What do you think of that?"
Matvei said it was something he always dreamed about; "but would the slips agree with this? And how much should he charge for getting the produce, and what would they sell in the actual store, and how much should he pay for the storage units, and the van? What about all that?"
Sam told him to think about it, weekly visits good or bad? How much to make it pay? What about if

there was no courtesy car? What do the slip people want?
You think about your stuff and when you are ready, I'll call a meeting of every one in here and then we can see if they like it or what changes they think of.
Mavei went off for most of a day in the courtesy car; at the end of the day he came back to Sam for a little get together.
"I've found a store that would provide our provisions; they will give me about a ten percent discount, sometimes a bit less, sometimes a bit more. I think that it would be all right to charge the slip owners ten or fifteen percent more for produce ordered by them and delivered to the boat. The things we could keep on the marina store would be things we could develop as time went by; but it would be things like milk, spreads like butter, each day I could bring vegetables, soon I think there could be a list of vegetable orders; we could see".
All right, if you're happy and we can get all our people for a meeting. Sam had some tables in the communion building, got some bottles of wine and some glasses and invited all slip holders for a meeting. He told the gathering that he wanted to tell them about a plan, with Mavei; he introduced the idea of a marina grocery shop with weekly visits for self-delivered groceries and a shop on

site for miscellaneous stuff. But I asked Mavei to look into it and I want to let him explain it to you, and I shall go off with Jess for a couple of hours. When he got back the meeting was over, he went to their boat to see what Mavei received from the meeting; Mavei had little to say.
"It was a lot to spring on a group just like that, I think they had questions to ask themselves about it. I told them how I thought it could work, but there was no real unified response."
"I think I might have a chat with some of the slip holders and see what they think."
So, he did, he had a long talk with Jess about it and decided to make this grocery talk be a part of a visit he had planned with some of his favorite people. And first of all, he visited Olive and Pat, his first slip people. He settled down on their settee with his big piece of coffee cake and a cup of hot chocolate; Jess was on the floor with a bit of his biscuit and they settled down for a long chat.
"I visit lots of the boats here, but it warms me here, with you two, more than any other boat; the air is warm with love, the furnishings are for the two of you share with more affection; it's so nice to be here, for me and Jess. We are lucky to be able to share it with you; you are lucky to have each other."

The girls sort of snuffled up to each other and held hands.
"Pat said, we have always felt comfortable with You Sam, we don't know why, perhaps it was because you welcomed us here when there was only us; but we value your friendship."
"Well," said Sam, "it's a very good thing to have friends. Or, another little thing, What did you think of Mavei's grocery story?"
"Olive said, well, we don't think he could make it pay, so if it started, we wonder if it would end as abruptly."
"You don't think it would pay him?"
"We don't think he can do it for the money."
"But Sam told them that it was likely that Mavei's price would have some discount and he could add something, like ten or fifteen percent and that would make him happy. I don't think wants to make a living at this, it just makes him happy in running his own grocery business with customers who are happy. That will make him happy."
With that Sam and Jess went on to another of their visits.
He joined Val and Francis and asked how they were getting along.
"Oh, we're wonderful," said Val," no problem for us; we go for a little walk about lunch time, after I've done some work, then when we come home

Francis has his lunch and goes to sleep and then I work some more."
"So Armond has plenty of work for you?"
"Yes, each time I submit work he assigns me more, right now I'm happy right here, well, until Francis reaches school age, then we can make a new arrangement, - - - perhaps," she said with a smile.
"I wanted to ask about this grocery business for the slips; what do you think?"
"Oh, not soon enough for me. All the baby stuff I have to get, nappies, wipes, ointments, all that stuff; it would be a very big help for me not to have to fuss over that every time. Oh yes, I can't wait for Mavei to begin."
"Well, you and the girls, I just have to ask a couple more and I can be happy.
Sam and Jess strolled around the dock until they came to Arthur's boat; he banged on the cabin top and Arthur looked out.
"Can I come and talk to you for a moment?" Asked Sam.
Arthur gave a little grin and held the washboards open.
Sam and Jess went down to see Duke, but also there was also Nancy from the ex-Long Island boat. She was settled on the settee with Duke beside her with his head on her lap.

"I didn't mean to interfere." Said Sam.
"No you didn't interfere," said Nancy, "we are having a late breakfast."
"A late breakfast; well; could I have some cinnamon toast and coffee, please."
Arthur reached for the toaster and put two slices of bread in, he got the coffee pot and poured a cup for Sam. When the toast was ready, he sprinkled sugar and cinnamon on and passed it to Sam.
"Actually," said Sam, "I really came to ask about the pre-ordered grocery plan, what you thought about it, what you would use it."
"Oh, we think it's great," they chorused, no need to spend time away from here, we think it's great and we will use it."
"That's OK," Sam told them, I think I'll get with Mavei to get started thank you, I've been to three people but I think I'll go and try Dave, but I think he would use it.
So, you two seem to have joined up in a sailor like way." He smiled with affection, "it seems like a sweet thing to do on boats, a very good thing for, the longing, but for the occasional loneliness and the need to have somebody to tell things too."
"And the loneliness of bedtime all alone." Said Nancy.
"Yes," said Sam, "no matter how you are, how old you might feel, having someone there to be

warm, to touch and to say nice things to in the middle of the night is a blessing. Well, I must go and see Dave, - - - - and, I wish you well in sharing your boats together, I really do."
And off he went, still feeling the still sorrowful gap left by Nina in his life.
He went below in Dave's boat and Sam and Jess said hello to Hobo, who rushed around in his serpentine, shambling route around the place; in the end Hobo went back to Dave's coat pocket and was quiet.
"What are you working on now Dave." Said Sam.
"I'm working on a John Harrison design; it's called a 'run silent' escapement, runs for twenty-six hours. This is for a clock, well, a clock sort of specialist who wants things that no one else has. I'm making the basic clock and I don't know, but I expect he will find some woodworker with more skills than me to make a cabinet for it. This is, for me, a bit special, I don't usually get stuff like this to work on."
"That will keep you engaged with new techniques to get to the design you need."
"Yes, it does."
"I came around to ask you what you thought about the grocery delivery idea."
"Wonderful, all the time I spend off here will be saved, very good idea! I hope it gets started soon."

The marina people had no bad vibes about Mavei's grocery plan, quite the reverse and so he told Mavei that tomorrow they could go to a second hand restaurant warehouse and fine the cold storage units he needed.
The next day Mavei and Sam went off to the warehouse that sold used kitchen and shop appliance hardware; there was a lot of stuff to look at, but finally Mavei selected a cold storage unit and a large refrigerator and three open air storage units. Sam asked some questions about expanding if need be and then asked the man about delivery and warrantee. Be delivered Thursday, warrantee for one year. They left quite excited.
The went on to the used car lot in their own village to look at a small van that Sam had looked at last week. They looked at it, drove it for a test drive, thought it was OK for the start-up of the service and Mavei drove it back to the marina. So that was that, for Sam, he let Mavei get on with it.
But now he had another project for Olive and Pat. He went again to visit with an expectation of coffee cake and dog biscuits. When he got settled with his victorious spoils, he told them he had a job for them.
"I wonder whether you two could find the time to do another marina thing; Marvei and I went to

buy the cold storage units for the shop, and the vegetable display counters; and we bought a used van for him to drive to get the groceries, so that might get started next week. Now there is another thing that I started but haven't got running and that is the big community building; in Addition to the grocery building, it is heated and airconditioned but it takes a couple to take it over and turn it into something we all enjoy. I have a vision of carpets, worn but attractive and nice on the floor, some table for four for bridge or other card games, other tables for two, for chess, or backgammon or whatever, a dartboard perhaps, I don't know what would be best, but I know something would make it, a couple of groups of armchairs around a coffee table. Well, I don't know what will work; but I wondered if you would take charge of it and get it running and, perhaps, keep it running. What do you think of that? Of course, I would pay for the furniture etc."

They agreed and Sam thought that in a couple of weeks there would be a community place for people to spend a couple of hours doing something that was beyond what they could do on their boat."

So in two or three weeks Olive and Pat invited him to look at what they had done; he held his breath as he walked up the path to the building; Pat stood at the door and opened it for him; he was very surprised at what they had done, not what they had done but how the bits and bobs had somehow come together to blend into the room that he had imagined. But not the room he had thought about but something better, a room that was more mature even though there was nobody in it. It was much better than he had imagined; what they had made was a room in which you would be happy, doing crosswords, playing chess, having quiet conversations, and, they had a little convenience counter with a kettle and all sorts to make tea, coffee, hot chocolates. There was a second hand fridge for beer and wine with and honor tray for payment. He looked at the tables, some table and, or chairs had been painted. The old carpets on the floor, the impressionist paintings on the walls, curtains for the windows. He turned to them.

"It is much, much better than I could have made it. We must have an opening. We just must have an opening.'

So, again Pat and Olive chose a date and an opening was scheduled that evening.

Sam attended and relished in the camaraderie between the slip holders; he smiled in satisfaction but went early with Jess back to his own boat. He almost all of his people, had some body to talk to, but increasingly he lost Giuirdre, Nina and Tina from his life. He went to bed early, thinking of what the marina could do for Christmas just three weeks away.

But just after breakfast the next day Pat and Olive came by to suggest that they organize and Christmas buffet in the companion building and so he got away from that and was looking forward to it.

It was a happy affair, dogs, ferrets, people, baby Francis were all there, the party went on long after Sam thought it would, Hobo was good, dogs lay in corners full with scraps torn off the grown up's dishes, people gathered to talk and the re-gathered with other people, and then again, there were no cliques, just boat people; and Sam was glad.

Chapter 12.—A New Life.

To burn always with this hard, gemlike flame,
To maintain this ecstasy, is success in life.
Walter Horatio Pater. The Renaissance, Conclusion.

New Year's came; but the boat people each did their own thing in their own boats; and when the New Year came the marina was quiet and peaceful by just after twelve. The weather was not too cold and the next day Sam was determined to get on with his housework. So, with Jess snoozing in his bed in the cockpit Sam was hoovering the cushions before vacuuming the sole. He was miles away with some thoughts, pushing the little vacuum cleaner about the settees when Jess broke into a very excited barking; and Sam got up from his knees and went out to see what it was that got Jess's attention. He climbed up the companionway and looked at the dock, oh, it was another dog like Jess that he was barking at, but as Sam climbed the last step to look at the dog, and he looked up further and there was Nina! Sam was aghast, he had no words; he looked at her, but didn't know what to do; he looked at Tina, playing with her old mate Jess; in the end he sat back on the seat locker and

still looked up at her. In the end he ventured a query.
"What are you doing down here Nina?"
She grinned at him. "When we parted at Giuirgre's house you said you loved me and wanted to go on forever. Well, I took you at your word; here I am, to be with you, if you still want me; and by the way; I have a hold all at the end of the dock and I rented a car to get here; so that car's gone as well."
Sam reached out a hand for her and then another hand for Tina. He took her tightly in his arms.
"You can ask Jess," he said, "but I have said most days that I wished you were here with me, my life has been empty of the things we used to do, the things we looked for, the things that might be far away in our lives, but most of all I missed the moonlight chats in our bed looking up at the sky, I missed you very much; and, here you are, are you here to stay?"
"Yes, Sam, here to stay if you want me."
"Come, with our dogs, we must go and get your hold all."
With the dogs they walked down the dock, at one boat they stopped and Sam said to the young woman.
"Val, this is Nina, my partner from before, now she has come home to join us again for ever and ever. Nina, this is Val, she lives here with her baby

Francis, and Val works for Arnold now like I do. We will see you soon, Val, when we get settled in."

And the next boat down Sam said.

"Olive and Pat, this is my partner Nina, come now to join me forever. Nina this is Olive and Pat, they were the very first one to come here to stay. We'll see you soon, perhaps we can have a party in your room."

So, they got Nina's hold all and Sam took it with him.

"Not wanting to lose this after all." He said.

Back at the boat with Tina and Sam playing in the cockpit they went below.

"You really are going to stay?" Asked Sam, "you really are going to stay?"

"Yes, I'm sorry for the difficulty that caused the break up before. I was looking after a brother who was born with spina bifida, his was untreatable, he needed looking after, I was the one to do that; the times I could be with you was when a local nurse could come. Now he is dead; so here I am, here to be with you."

"Yes, but are you going to stay. I would not want to go through all that again."

"Yes, I'm going to stay; so, you can show me how to put all my things and also for Tinas, she'll be staying too you know."

They went on, putting her things away, some in the bathroom, some in the living areas, and some in the bedroom aft of the cockpit, Tina had her place for her food and for the foldup bed Nina had brought for her. At last they went for a walk for the dogs so that they could have an uninterrupted evening. As they set off from the boat Nina said.
"Do you like living in this marina, amongst all these people?"
"No, it is not that, you remember when I introduced Olive and Pat as the first to come here? Well this is my marina, all of it. I bought it when it was just the piers and the walkways, from a lady who wanted to get rid of it; so all the rest is mine and these are my people, they are all my friends; the self-delivery grocery service was my idea and the communion house was my idea; so it is a little mobile boat community. I liked it as I was getting it started and built up but more lately, I have lost my way a bit; but now with you here it will be back to what it used to be."
"You have all this? You must have difficulty paying for all this."
"Well, something happened to me about the time we parted; I didn't get it to talk to you about it because we were not together; anyway, I won a lot of money on the state lottery system, and that's all that I have spent here."
"Oh, that's a lot. All of this is yours"

"Well, I still work for Armond the way I used to; but now, I don't know, the work is harder than it was; I haven't asked Armond about it, whether it's hard or times are changing. I have to see what's in his mind, but anyway, now you're here I'm going to forget it for a bit."

"Now my visiting-but-staying-angel we need to have a shower and there is only room for one at a time; I really like you to go second, but tonight it might be best if you went first and I can make sure you have all you need."

The aft room was suitable: the both dogs were settled down as they used to, in times past, there were towels for Nina when she was finished, Sam sat waiting on the little built-in chair. Sam waited and thought; his mind swirled with two big thoughts: was Nina really going to stay? But this was on the fringes of his mind as he waited to see her again after all this time; did he remember her well? The grace she had when she said she agreed with something; the sweep in her body as she reached up to her hair, the cheeky look in her face as she turned towards him. And then the shower door opened and she took a step over the edge; and she was more lovely than he could remember. But; she held up both hands in a defensive mode and shooed him into the shower whilst she hurried off to bed. He hurried up with

his shower and dried off, put out the light and went to the bed.
"Just like the very first night," Nina said, "to lay with hand holding and talk about the future."
And they lay, Sam with her hand held tightly and snuggled up close to her; they looked out the same old hatch they used to look through, Sam turned to her and asked.
"Are you really, really going to stay?"
"Yes, if you want me, I will stay."
Then their night grew into a long, loving and tumultuous evening that went on until the small hours, until they drifted off into peaceful sleep.
In the morning they had a long breakfast; Nina was finding out where all the kitchen things were and Sam was relishing the company, he had for so long been lonesome for. He had decided not to work today and had texted Armond to tell him that; but Armond, in a way that had been increasing over the past few months, agreeing grudgingly. Sam mentioned to Nina, over their second cup of coffee, that Armond did not have the way of dealing with things the way he used to have.
"I'll have to have a chat with him sometime soon to see what's going on with him."
But their life came together in their new engagement. Sam took Nina to meet all the slip owners in their own homes: Olive and Pat, now

understood by Nina, Val with Francis where Nina spent most of their visit playing with him, Arthur and Nancy with their late-in-life bloom of affection, Olga and Mazei in charge of provisions, the repairman, who showed her his clock and all the rest of what he called to her his people. They took the courtesy car and went off for the day to buy wine and other secret delights.

But still in all of this Sam was not still in his mind about life here with Nina, it just wasn't going to be permanent, not especially for Nina, far from the things she knew about. So, what about Nina, what must he do, something, but he could not make any decision, he had to make some changes.

After lunch they went to the village for odds and ends and Sam had to visit the mail box in the post office.

"I don't get very much mail, the electricity bill and such like but that is about it."

But today he brought back a large envelope with three re-numbered addresses on it, he said he must open it; he slit the envelope and pulled out the contents. He read it and he read it again, then he turned to Nina and said.

"Giuirdre has left me her house, that house, we know by the river, she left me her house."

Sam began to have tears running down his face, he sobbed, "it was for us, you and me, it was for us, for us to live our lives in."

His tears continued to roll; Nina took his head in her arms but said nothing. He was still but his head with Nina's. At last he straightened up and said with a patient voice.

"That seals my mind you know; I have been wondering how we could make a life, but here would not work, not for the two of us, but to go home, where we met, and make a life in Giuirdre's house, that lifts me up very well, that makes me happy, for the both of us."

He sighed, but went on, "I'll have to sell the marina," but he went on with a smile, "but only to the slip holders you see; I've thought about it before, sell each person the slip they are in but, along with all the others, each slip owner will have an equal share in the rest of the marina, the marina will be a development with all the slip owners having an equal interest. That's what I will do, talk to the lawyer and call the slip owners for a meeting to brief them."

So, in the next few days he went to the lawyer to see if his plan was real and then spend time making up a list of things that could be the start of the operating plans for a development marina. In a few more days, he called the slip owners to a meeting in the community house. When they were all there, he stood on a milk box and raised his arms.

“You will remember we had a meeting about the grocery supplies and then we had a meeting about this community room, they were successful meetings and this is another one; this is one that is going to have some impact on your lives. Something has happened in my life, something that I must heed. The result is that I need to sell this marina.” But Sam held his hands up high. “But nothing bad, I hope, my plan is to sell it all to you. First of all, I’m only going to take out the money I have in it. Second my plan, which I offer to you is that; the marina will be sold as a development corporation, each one of you will be a stockholder. Each one of you will pay for the slip you will own, but you will also have a one-nineteenth share in the rest of the marina. So, you will have to vote once every few years for a chief person and you should also vote on say four or six persons as board members. Your dues, that have been paid to me will not be needed, but some will be put in the marina for repairs and annual costs like insurance and real estate taxes. On the table by the door are copies of some of the things I suggest you need to put in your operating plan. The lawyer will help with that. There are eighteen slips, two are unoccupied so I need $10,000 for each slip. That will get you your slip and a one twentieth share of the marina; that is like less than two years rental for your slip.

You can talk among yourselves, if some among you are too short of money, I think others will help you out. I have also talked to the manager of the bank here in town and he will probably give a personal loan. I want all this done by the end of next week and there will be a settlement then. The settlement will be between me and a development you can name for your own home. I can leave you here to discuss this, and, you need a chief person and tree board members to sign for receiving the purchase."

Sam and Nina left to go back to their boat. Nina thought Sam had made a good job of explaining things and they just took the dogs for a walk and then went to bed.

In a couple of days' time five owners came to visit: Arthur was president and Nancy, Olive, Pat and Dave were there. They settled down on the settees and Arthur said they could raise all the money and the slip owners were all happy to have been able to have a part of it. They said they had been to visit the lawyer and to do the things that will be required to make the settlement go well. Sam told them that he had already had a title search for the marina, but said they could have one done if they wanted. He said that he would sign the titles for the courtesy car and the grocery van and he would sign the title for the marina at the time of settlement. He said he would send a letter to the insurance company and the electric company. And he asked that the slip owners get a cashier's check for him at settlement. And he concluded by saying he was very glad that they had got together to keep the community the way it was. Arthur said they were, separately, going to put together a list of rules and laws for the forward operating of the marina. A date was set for the settlement and the meeting ended.

Sam and Nina now had to plan the next part of their lives

Chapter 13.Begin --A New Life.

All rising to a great place is by a winding stair.
Francis Bacon. *Of a Great Place.*

Sam said he could go alone but Nina could come if she wanted to be with him and the boat. This caused a very animated and vigorous response from Nina and they settled down to plan it together.
Sam said that some offshore sailing will be required whichever way they go, and he suggested that they go inland up to Norfolk and then go offshore all the way home. He told Nina that alternately they could go up to Cape May and up the New Jersey coast to the East River and then by the Cape Cod canal and home by a shore bound route. She favored the offshore route to get home quicker, and for the dogs, but suggested that when they got offshore by New Jersey they would watch the weather and make a final decision.
The next week they planned their provisions, They planned and schemed and bought food to put in the fridge and food to keep dry and food for the dogs. Nina packed it all away while Sam made notes in an exercise book for them to share on the way home. The more he thought about it the

more he thought about taking the inland route, better for the dogs, places to rest if they thought so, pressure to the land when they got through the Cape Cod canal, eventually he told Nina who was glad of his decision; so they settled back with that plan; to get "Home" as soon as they could. The settlement was a smooth and, on both sides, a bitter-sweet exchange of the points of view, the new marina managers were very keen to do a great job of running things, but there was not very much to do except keep it clean and functioning. But Sam smiled. "In time there will be changes or expansions you will want to consider, you'll have things to talk about, you'll see."

So, Sam went to the bank on his way home and deposited the check; the he hurried back to Nina to set a day and time for their departure.

They left on a Monday morning right after breakfast. All the slip owners came out to wish them well, Sam was aware that it was a part of his life that would not come again, but the wholeheartedness of the boat owners brought tears to his eyes, he and Nina waved goodbye until they were hidden by the turn in the river. Then they turned their hopes to their journey together and their hopes of home.

Sam had thought about the trip and set out the day's journey so that they could be alone and have a place for the dogs to run, mostly it worked like that.

They had some things to do, to continue to get ready and so they made a short run and anchored at Haystack Point, got all their stuff in order and then went in with the dinghy and found space for the dogs to run for an hour. Then back to the boat for a late lunch and an early night and then off to shore for a brief dog run and then the first real day's journey, well, not a large one; they anchored again off Tuckahoe Point and had another restful evening. They had another restful day and stopped at the Coinjock marina for a meal and a place for the dogs. The next day was a longer day and they left at the first light and went through Portsmouth and Norfolk to anchor at Mile Post one for a not very restful evening.

A rough ride the next days across the Brown's Bay in Mobjack Bay.

And so up the Chesapeake Bay: Fishing Bay, Solomons, a long way to the West River and another day of motoring to Still Pond Creek. Sam said they would rest here in the shelter of the long farmland.

"I stayed here with Jess on the way down; there is a long beach to walk along, nice little rocks to have a little grill and peaceful, very peaceful here; just no lights, a place to see the sky and, well, Jess and I were sorry to leave, and then, in memoriam, we were a good bit sad for the lives we had left behind."

So here they stayed for three days, mostly all alone, big walks along the beach twice or three times a day, and once, when the wind had dropped and the sun was out, they grilled steaks over a driftwood fire.

And so as they got closer to home they hurried onwards: Chesapeake City and then to Delaware City to wait for the Delaware River tides to help them on to Cape May, then to Atlantic City, up to Sandy Hook and then the exciting East River, a rest along the Cape Cod canal and then a burst out into the ocean a few hours from home.

The last bit of their journey was in silence; then they turned the last bend and they could see the dock. Sam powered back, approaching at just about idle speed, put the boat in steerage way and came up to the dock. Nina leapt ashore and tied up; the dogs were next, sniffing and peeing, Sam shut off the engine and went ashore with Nina.

"Let's go and see what will be our home."

They held hands; they could see the garden that used to give Giuirdre pleasure, the flower beds that gave her so much contentment were all grown over with last year's plants and the foliage of the old summer; but still, it was all there. They strolled up the gravel path that Sam had laid, but it seemed that it could be made good again; they turned the corner and could see the house, the path was no better here, but the garden shed with the sun shade looked in good shape. The garden beds in front of the house were full of wizened blooms and tall tangled and ragged Foxgloves against the building. The house looked very well but cobwebs and spiderwebs were all over the windows and the front door.

"The letter said the key is in the garden shed." Said Sam as he walked towards the shed door.

He went in and came out with the front door key. They walked to the door together.

Sam inserted the key and pushed the door open. He said. "I want to see the kitchen. "

They both went into the kitchen. There on the old table was two envelopes; one from Giuirdre's daughter, Sam opened that first. They looked at it together.

"Look it's just a note telling us that Giuirdre's family were happy with our having the house, Giuirdre had plenty of other things for her family and they were happy that after all the time we spent with her it was just that we could go on living in her memory." Sam opened the second note, they were both surprised, it was from Giuirdre, nicely written in her black decisive hand.

"Well," he said, "it said that the three or more years you and I spent with her was the best of her life. After the Christmas we spent here was when she wrote this letter, and she hopes that you and I, together, will carry on, living here, making a family and thinking of her as we do that."

Nina put her arms around his shoulder as his eyes filled with tears.

"I shall keep this letter forever." He said.

They waked back to the boat and then took the dogs for their promised walk. Sam was silent, not the usual 'look at this - - look at that' they walked home again and Nina got a meal and they sat down to eat; Sam still did not say much. When Nina had put everything away and came back to Sam he got her to sit on the settee and he knelt beside her on the sole. He took her both hands in his and said there were two things he wanted to ask her about. She sat quiet and paid attention.

"First," Sam said, "Nina will you marry me?"

Nina leaned forward and lowered her head on to his.

"Of course, I will marry you. I came all the way down looking for you, and you know, Armond was the only person I could find who knew where you were. And what is this second thing?"

Sam turned a bit red, but pressed on.

"Can you do what it is you do so we can have a baby, or two?"

"Of course Sam, two would be quick, close together, we can all grow up together."

"Yes, I'd like that very much; we can do what we want to Giuirdre's house; it will be our house but I will always feel that she was there, with us, like the Christmases we were there with her, we will all be there with her. And tomorrow I can go and get my old car and have this chat with Armond whatever he has to say."

So, back where they began, hand in hand in their bed looking up at the sky, with the dogs sniffling about getting settled for the evening.

Nina came to bed, with her little news.

"I have put away my little pot, today we will begin to count the days for a baby. So, you had better get started my man."

And they did.

The next day after breakfast Sam went to fetch his car from the resting place in Arnold's barn. When the taxi had dropped him off he found, to his great delight that Arnold, or somebody he had hired, had taken his car to be washed, have a new battery and was, as Sam's car was able, to go about their daily business.

Sam knocked on Arnold's door and went on in. Arnold was busy with some phone conversation with an employee or a customer. Sam sat and read a magazine until Arnold was finished.

"So, my friend Arnold, what is it that makes you want a face to face discussion? Are you going to fire me?"

Arnold pushed back his chair and lit one of his long thin cigars. He pondered, gathering up his line of thought.

"This business has got big. Not big like it used to be when we started, but big. I have been wondering, while you were away, to sell, to get a partner, get more help or what to do. I still don't know. If I sell it or get someone to help; that has the appearance to have given away your daughter to a rascal from the next village. I keep coming back to one of two choices: sell out and make our about twenty software designers, maybe redundant or at least at risk. The other way is to get a trusted and loyal friend to join me in the business, and you would come to mind, and split the work in the way that would work for the two of us. We would have to talk about this; what you would get out, what you would put in and what share you would have in the fortunes of the company. I wanted to tell you that. I have an outline in my mind, but I want you to think about it and tell me what you think. Say next Tuesday or Wednesday.

And then, this cigar is drawing very nicely so I'll let you go and think about it."

Sam did think about it on his way home, about how it would be for him, working that way, and how it would be for the wife-to-be and the two daughters thereafter. He knew Arnold did not know of the benevolence of Giuirdre's house and he did not know of the state lottery win. He believed Arnold thought he had the money he got when he sold his apartment long ago; so, what did Arnold expect from him?

He got home and parked his shiny not so new car and went down to Nina. He wrapped her in his arms once again.

"So long to be away from you; awful it has been. I ache with loneliness; can we go to bed for a while?"

"Well, all right if you want to. I took the dogs for a walk so they're all right."

So; the dogs were OK, Sam was content too; Nina was content in Sam's arms and, snuggled up to him, asked.

"So, what did Arnold want?"

"I'm not entirely sure; but I think he wants me for a partner; perhaps not an equal partner, but the business has grown beyond the reach of one man, even for Arnold. He could sell the business but that would place all his software designers at risk. You see just like me, all his employees are remote workers and working in ways that suit them. Some work twenty hours a week, some work sixty hours a week; and he has some measure of what each one does and they're paid for what they have done. I'm not sure how he has that worked out, but he can do it. But he asked me what kind of

arrangement and I don't know. He doesn't know we have this house, and he doesn't know about my lottery win; so, he must think I just have the money I got from selling my apartment a long time ago,
And I don't know does he still own the business? And if he did, what part could I play and what would I get out of it. Any even more; do we want something like that with a married wife and two daughters? Tell me that." He said as he laughed with his face on her neck. "Behave yourself," Nina laughed, "Arnold has the business for what is it? Sixteen years and you worked for him all that time and you can't say much about it? No overhead, no buildings except the one he lives in. He has good benefits for his workers. I believe you do have an idea how it all works and you are looking for my suggestion for the future. I don't know, but I suggest you think of a going in position; say put in one hundred and fifty thousand and see what he said and get him to tell you how the company is owned and what part you would play in that. And, you know, there may be the first sister to think of."
"All right, that's a plan, I'll go back Monday and see what he says. Now, we must spend time looking at our home to make it work for a wife and two children."

They took the dogs and went back to the house. Before they went in again Sam asked.
"Are you happy about having this for our house, forever?"
Nina looked at him.
"We met here, grew together here, we have the memories of our friend Giuirdre, we will be married soon, we hope to have babies soon, you have work to do and a future; and you ask me if I am happy! I am ecstatic that's what I am; so, come on, let's go inside and begin to plan.
They went in and Sam said they would go back to the kitchen where they had memories and begin to share thoughts there.
"This is the place we can share, but it is your place. Tell what you want it to be."
"I love it here, where Giuirdre made cakes, scones, big cooked dinners for Christmas; I want to keep the spirit; but for the future, with tiny children; I suppose the counter overlooking the garden would be replaced by a modern one with a wipe down top, maybe the other counter can be replaced to match. I like the wood-stove, we can get a fireguard and it will be nice in winter. The old quarry tiles are damaged, we could have new ones; but I don't want to lose the thoughts and memories."
They went on through the house, first Sam said air conditioning all over. New double pane windows,

probably more attic insulation, a room for Sam to work, the upstairs old bathroom would be kept with a refinished sink, bathtub and a bidet. Another bathroom downstairs. They said that each room they would have a joint review of colors, carpets etc.,
So, they had a look around but didn't decide much; they had the boat anyway.
Monday Sam went off to Tom, a friend of his who ran a building business they made arrangements for a visit in two days' time. Then he had a visit with Arnold, what might that bring?
He knocks on the door of Arnold's work rooms and went in. Again, Arnold was busy again with some business and Sam waited until he was finished.
"Well," Sam said, "I am here to see if we can agree on what I can do to relieve you of some of your torments," he laughed, "and for all these years I thought you were happy with your company. Before I make an offer, I need to know who owns the business and what part I can be in that." Arnold smiled.
"OK the business is all mine. You sold all your stock when it was convenient to you, most of the other stock were purchased by me later on, a bit at a time. But it is all mine now."
"Well," asked Sam, "is there an entity, a development, or company?"

"Of course there is; that's what protects the rest of our property from debts the company acquires."
"Oh, so what part might I play in the company?"
"Well, that depends on what you have a mind to do. If, for example, you bought in, then you would become a shareholder; and you would be entitled to a share of the profits."
"And what might be the share of profits in relation to the buy in share?"
Arnold paused for a moment and then he said.
"The company has no material assets, it's just me operating here. I run about twenty two software designers who work according to their own needs, well, most of the time. I check their own time cards and I have never been had, yet. I have an accountant who views the cards every week and pays the people. So, there is nothing to require a buy in, only me because a buy in would go right into my bank. So, for me the issue is how much of a buy in and how much can I pay annually.
I know you of old and having you for a partner has a lot of appeal. For you a buy in of one hundred and fifty thousand would buy forty five percent of the business. That would be an annual income, based on past years, of about a hundred and eighty thousand dollars. We would need to thrash out the details, particularly work sharing, we would need to meet here once a week and we

both need to work out some details of the arrangement. So that's my offer. Go away and think about it and come back within the week to go forward or stop."

Sam thought of Nina and the house where they were to live, and, in the future, some children that looked like Nina. He thought Arnold's offer went back to long ago, when he sold his flat; he thought Arnold's offer assumed he still had that flat money and whether he thought that would draw him in; he was right, it was enough to attract him, providing the rest of the arrangements provided the right working and legal arrangements he thought it was good for him.

When he got home, Nina had the dogs quiet in the cockpit and she took his hand and took him back into their room and gently took off his clothes put him to bed and joined him there.

"You can tell me first, or last," she laughed, "but you have to tell me."

"First," said Sam, "tell you first and then drift off into far off lands.

Well, we didn't talk much, just feeling our way in. In the end, which was not far in coming, Arnold offered to sell me forty five percent of the company for a hundred and fifty thousand dollars, and based on past years books, this would pay about a hundred and eighty thousand dollars each year. There will be some procedure and legal stuff to put in place, we will meet once a week at his place but that's about it. Much like you and I talked about before I went."

"Why does he want to sell it?"

"He doesn't; but only to me. The business has grown too large for him, to sell or take on a partner would put the lives of his staff at risk, this means he can go on without giving up but only sharing with someone who thinks like he does. So, if you agree I shall move it along and if the details can be OK, we'll be software business owners."

"OK now you have got all that off your mind you can give attention to the first of your children. Oh! And by the way, can we pick a day for our wedding?"

Chapter 14.—The House and the Wife.

My love is the maid ov all maidens,
Though all mid be comely.
William Barnes. In the Spring.

The next day Tom came by and Sam and Nina spent most of the morning with him. Tom finally said.

"I'll go off and make a start; estimates for the kitchen, air conditioning and window replacement. We'll get that finished or at least underway before we can identify more work."

That was done. Sam went to Arnold's and they worked out their arrangement; Sam went to a lawyer and resolved his concerns for the future. Sam and Nina went on to become equal partners and Sam and Arnold launched their joint procedure, with the work and staff assigned as suited them and their weekly meeting turning into a lunch business meeting.

The work on the house went according to Sam's cost and schedules so work proceeded on other rooms. Sam left Nina to do as she wanted; but in other rooms he took a strong interest; his work room was set up as he had always wanted; with modern desks and bookcases; he devoted part of his room space to provide a downstairs small bathroom with a small shower stall. For the upstairs bathroom, he got a very professional bath, sink and toilet refinisher and got a bidet for them to match too, and a very fine job it was; he enjoyed for many years the quiet loveliness of the bathroom and its fittings. The finishing of the walls and the fittings were made to match. He called Nina in to see it when it was finished and he told her to buy towels and other stuff to make it what he wanted it to be when they finally decided to live in the house. They both had, unstated, a strong desire to stay in the boat that was their first home.

Other things went ahead. Their wedding was a quiet festival of Sam, Nina and some friends: Arnold, Katy and their four children, Joyce, the daughter of Giuirde with her husband and daughter, two of Nina's friends from school, and two of Sam's sailing friends from the old times. They were married in the church where Nina's spina bifida brother was buried. Their reception was in Arnold's barn and it was a time of happiness with all the people there.

About six weeks later Nina came to Sam as he was in his work with a pink plastic thing in her fingers. "Here," she said in great seriousness, "is the first of our children. Born in the gravity of birth control pills and as ordered by the Software Master."

Sam took her onto his lap and laid his head on her breast.

"I suppose we had better get Tom to finish the house then," and he looked at her,
"mustn't we?"
And so, room by room they got the house ready for a family and not a bunch of teenagers; most rooms were ready move along whenever they felt like it.
Time passed; Nina found a lady doctor who looked after her and the first child; Nina and Sam were quite clear that this was the first, of, what was for Nina, a small tribe, and for Sam daughters of Nina to spread his love over.
Time came for an ultrasound.
"What shall we do." Asked Nina. "See what we got in there.?"
"Of course," said Sam, "then we can choose names."
So, Nina did. It was a girl. Sam knew that it was to be from the first moment.
"Sam said we must be very careful, for names, very careful. I want you to choose names because you are better at that; but, I want it to have two names and the middle one starts with a 'G' for Giuirdre, in fact all children's names like that, even if it is just you and I that know why"
One day Nina got a call from Katy, Arnold's wife; they had not had much to do with them socially so Nina was a little surprised.

"When you are next going to town, could we meet for a cup of coffee?" Asked Katy.

"Sure," responded Nina, "in fact I'm coming in on Thursday for a visit to my doctor, could we meet after that? Say eleven?"

Later Nina told Sam about the call, but he had no idea either, except that Katy might want to have someone in the younger set to talk to.

Anyway, Thursday came and after Nina's doctor visit, they met up.

"I expect you wonder why I called you," said Katy, "it was for me to just tell you about our husband's arrangement. You see, Arnold was single when I met him," she laughed, "I would have to have been the one to meet him, he was just about writing programs, so I prized him away from that, in time to seduce him and marry him. Well, he really hasn't changed, except that in addition to me loving him he has four other kids as well. But time passes and things fall into place, the work was important to pay for all of us, but then the work became more, then more; and he didn't have time for us, not the way he wanted to. But then, but then he thought of Sam. Well I couldn't get him in gear quick enough but in the end he did; and Sam joined him.

And I wanted to be with you to tell you that in the five months of that Arnold has become a different man, a very different man. Time now he has for

the children and time he has," and she blushed here, "time enough for me at night and now I have some fetching negligees and" again some redder blushes, "some other interesting, mutually interesting, stuff as well.
So, I wanted to tell you how your Sam has transformed our lives; transformed I say, because he joined up with Arnie. Thank you and him so much; I hope Sam has got satisfaction from his part."
"Yes, he has, I think his work has changed from being a task, an interesting task, to one more of owning something, with the task still involved; yes, I think it has been good for him too."
They left with promises to meet again soon and talk of wider things and not just husbands.
Over lunch Nina told Sam about her visit, in great detail to satisfy him, about her visit to the doctor's. And then told him the story about Arnie, Katy, the negligee and the sex toys and the way that their lives have been changed by Arnie's relief from the work that had got too much. She told Sam that she would be having some time with Katy and it felt good to her to have a friend like that to meet up with.
"Sam was glad that Arnie was happier in his work and he said that he was happier too. He said that he had been thinking about getting to know the people who worked for them, but Arnie said that

would not be good; he had tried that early on in his career but it had not been a success with various sorts of problems arising that would have otherwise laid dormant. So, Sam was not going to try it either.

Then Sam said

"Do you remember Val? The woman in one of our slips? The woman with a baby?

Well, she sold her slip, for thee times what she paid us, and wants to move up here somewhere; a place where she could send her son to school and all that. She would like to buy a slip like she had down there; but that isn't going to work up here. But she still wants to work for us so that's all right.'

But lunch was over and Sam had to go back to work. Nina did not have much to do;

She so she went to look at one of the two nursery rooms; that they had decided to be for the first child. But as she looked, it was a bit of a persuasive, not forceful look at things; she stood looking past her nursery room to the life she had led after high school: looking after her brother, a hopeless task and one of which she liked less as time went on. She didn't have time for more education, hobbies, nothing, until she found a way to have Tina and met Sam. Nothing, she could do nothing; she couldn't face the rest of her life

doing nothing except raising children. But what could she do?
She ran to her phone and called Katy, the only one she could ask about such things.
"What do you do, except look after your kids?"
"I potter a bit. Before I became fit with child, many years ago; I pretended to be a potter; Arnie fixed me up with a workshop out in the barn and I play out there. Of course, two are in school and there will be one more for the next two years and then I can have time to play again. What about you?"
"I became a child minder when I left school, it wasn't until a year or so ago that my brother died. So, I have no potters or anything, I keep wondering about myself. I thought I would call you."
"There must be something you'd like to do?"
"I'd like going to bed with Sam."
"Yes, of course. But for yourself, do you take photographs, doing stitching, anything, is there nothing you'd like to do?"
"I was good at art in school."
"Well, there you are! I shall find an art class for you, probably find one that you can take a baby too later on. Leave it to me."
And she did. And she did well. The next week Nina went on her own to talk to one of the teachers. The class was only two weeks old and they met

twice a week, she walked around the class and there, lo and behold, a baby n a carry cot. She got a list of equipment and rushed off to tell Sam. The first class for Nina was in two days. She rushed to see Sam and fell over herself telling him of her conversation with Katy and now she had been and signed up.

"I'm very glad of that," Sam said, "I have been worried since we came back and I couldn't see anything except babies, I didn't like that but I couldn't see anything else. But this, this will expose you to a new set of people, artists, writers, musicians, just all sorts. But, he said, you have to invite me to all the things you take part in. Yes, I think it is a very good idea and this seems to be the right time to buy a second car. Can we go to bed for a while my artist?"

"Any time, that's what I told Katy, going to bed with you was my best thing."

Chapter 15.— An Advent of Artist.

Rules and models destroy genius and art.

William Hazlitt. On Disagreeable people On Taste.

Sam took them out to buy another car, not a new one, but a good one. One with places for artist's easels, paints and canvases and, many baby implements. Sam got Nina to go for a long test drive, without him, and as she was happy, they went home in a car each.
The next day she went to the artist's shop and bought all that was on her list. Now the next day she was off to her first class.
She went in and was met by Andy, the teacher.
"What happened to the list of materials I gave you?"
"There all in the car, I didn't know what to bring in."
"Did you buy a storage case?"
"Yes, I bought everything you told me."
"Come on then, we'll go out to your car and get ready for your first lesson."
He took the things she would need and then led her into the school. He introduced her to the rest of the students, found her a place and told her to

set up her easel, attach some paper and he would be back in a moment to get her started.
He went around to the other students and came back to her.
"OK, there's your canvas, here, use this Conté stick. Draw me something, anything."
This wasn't anything she imagined, drawing anything; for him! She came to be taught. She didn't know what to draw. "Come on," he said, "draw anything."
She looked around to find something to draw; over there was a student, sort of different, dressed in bib and brace coveralls, bent over her canvas. Nina stood looking at her and then, because she had to draw, she, in a very few strokes, drew this lady; involved, encompassed, and poised; an artist involved at her work.
The teacher looked at her work. He looked at her. He said I know not what to say.
"I can't teach you anything, you're a better artist than me. Now look here, there's this group of artists that meet right here on Monday nights, at six thirty. You really should come and meet the people there, they will tell you, offer you some place to go and how to grow your skills, but don't come here; you will cause these artists to be afraid to work, don't come here. Now; I'll see you on Monday, OK?"

She packed up her stuff and went home to Sam, Jess and Tina. She plopped on the deck and down into the family.
"Well?" Said Sam, "you're home early what happened.?"
"He threw me out," Nina replied, "told me not to stay there; I would make the other students miserable. Told me about another group of real artists that meet on Mondays, same place. I have to go and meet them on Monday."
"Not very much surprised," remarked Sam, "I have seen some of your sketches. Maybe this time you'll get some help."
As they cuddled up together that night, she had a half of an idea, the next morning she called Katy and asked if she could come in and see her.
She got up early and told Sam she was going to Katy's house. She was there early and was a part of getting the children ready to play and then she asked Katy if she had some work in her workshop. The au pair girl took the children and went off to the playground. Katy took Nina out to her work room. Nina said she wanted to see work that was not finished. Katy showed her some vases in various shapes and sizes. Nina looked at the tall slender vases; there were three there that were finished but not fired.
"What kind of paint is required for firing this kind of vase?" Asked Nina.

"There are all kinds." Said Katy. There are a few here but the art store has plenty more."
"What about when you want a background and then put more on it, perhaps several colors?"
"Just the same."
"I could get some colors, whatever I wanted. Could you make me some vases, I would like to make some with colors and designs; would you fire them for me?"
"Oh, yes, that would be fun, you take these and get some paints at the store, give me a call before you bring them back."
Nina took the three vases and went to the store and asked where was the paints for firing vases. She looked over and picked some background colors and half a dozen primary colors and hurried off home. She went to the room that Sam had picked for her work for herself room and looked at the three vases. She stood the first one on a plastic table and studied it. She decided what background color and took a foam brush. Without much trouble she painted the whole outside and as far down inside as she could reach. She thought that was all right and proceeded to paint the next one a different color and the third one. All seemed all right so she called Katy and asked if she could come tomorrow to get them fired.
Meanwhile she played with some ideas for decoration; the one vase was tall, slender so she

would have an all black tall and slender dancer, another, also tall, she thought to have an ex-libris motif of some kind and the last vase was flat like a small decanter and she would paint some half full wines with matching stoppers.
She was here lost in her work until Sam came looking for her, he looked at the background and the three designs and said it would be a bit of a job getting her to look after a child. She laughed.
"I don't have one yet, and when I do it will be first on my list like you are Sam."
And she pulled him on to her lap and told him all the things they would do after the dogs had taken them for a walk and had their dinner.
The next morning, she took her vases to Katy and had her explain all she was going to do and how Katy explained they might come out.
"It's a bit of a risk," she explained, "sometimes it just doesn't come true, no matter what you do."
She was going to heat up and cool slowly so the vases would not be ready until tomorrow. They had a coffee and morning chat and their friendship was growing with the child coming for Nina and now, possibly some connection with Katy's sculptures.
The next day, after lunch, Nina went to Katy. The vases were on her table and looked fine to Nina.
"There are not really as good as it be to sell them; but they are OK for your art project aren't they?"

“Yes, they are; I wonder if I can bring them back tomorrow, decorated, could I have them by Monday afternoon? I have a meeting to go to and I want to have something to show them.”
“Yes, why not? You bring them back tomorrow and we’ll, see; and good luck with your work.”
She got home and went to Sam’s work area; he was working on a Saturday.
“You’re in charge of getting lunch Sam, I have to work; you can bring mine up to me in my studio I have to get some vases back to Katy tomorrow so I can take them to this meeting on Monday night - - - OK?”
She went to her room. Which design should be first? She thought about that. She felt in her mind that she wanted the all-black tall dancer - - like the designs that
René Lalique made – Art Nouveau - - - those magique times in art, and like the Blue Nudes of Henri Matisse. Oh, she was being carried away by her dreams, best to start. She stood the vase on her plastic table and mixed some very black paint. She stood looking at the vase and decided one figure each side would be right.
She chose her brush, immersed the bristles in her paint and did an image all of about three strokes and ceased. She turned the vase on the table, get more paint and drew a second image, similar to the first but not the same. She looked at her work

and decided it was the best she could do with the skills she had.
For the second vase she had thought that a design each side would be good also. She had in her mind an ex-libris design, after the swirls and shapes of maidens, holding the design, holding the design of a book place. She decided to put the image in an ornate frame. She set out and made the frame and, in another color, sketched the image of the ex-libris maid. That was all right too.
The last vase she had thought about a half-filled decanter, filled with sexy deep red wine, the same sort of look from all sides.
When she was done the day was dark and her sandwich was still uneaten. Still, she was happy and that was what it was about.
She took her sandwiches back to Sam; he smiled and said.
"You were so much involved with your work; I didn't like to distract you, I left the sandwiches for when you woke up, but I can see you didn't wake up. And do you know what I think? I think it is very good, very good for you having this come into your life, and, good for me, not having to think of you drifting, without having a lead of something to draw you along. I think it is all very encompassing for the two of us. Now, come on I took the dogs out so you can have a glass of wine and then - - - - ."

The next day she was back at Katy's house for the firing. Katy looked at the designs for a while and said.
"These would fetch a very good price in some high value pottery shop."
Nina said. "Well, why don't you open one? Your kids do not want too much of your time. Get Arnold to look into it. Anyway, could I have these after lunch tomorrow? I think I will take two of these with me to my meeting with the art people - - - see what they have to say."
The next day Katy showed the glazed vases. Katy looked at them; Nina looked at them. Nina looked at Katy.
"Well, are they OK? Would you offer them for sale? Well, what do you think?"
Katy said. "They are good. The art work is very good. If our plan was to make more of these for sale, then the vase finish would be better, quite a bit better. But I think I could do that, make it more smooth, able to take the finish better. But, all in all, these are three vases that we can stand behind. I will wait to hear what your 'Experts" have to say; but if you want, we could possibly share a small store in somewhere where people go who would appreciate this, not any old place, a place such people go. I don't know just where to look, but we can if you want."

Nina had a dinner with Sam that he made. "No wine," he said, "before your meeting; But - - - - when we come home, well, nice hot shower for you and a Greek cheese, home-made bread - - warm and wine and maybe Ouzo; have to see; meanwhile; off you go in your car with your work."
So, she did; off you go she said to herself as she went, vases in her canvas cover, hopes high, but not too high. The place where they were to meet was the staff room of the college where she had gone for art lessons; now it was to meet with the lords of all that.
She went in and found her way there; her ex-teacher, Andy, was there and he indicated to sit beside him. When all were there, her teacher rose and said to them that he had got Nina to come for a visit; he said she came to his art class but he couldn't let her stay because of the other students work; in fact, he told them that her twenty seconds work display was better work than he would ever do. I invited her to come and talk to you all. I asked her to bring some work to show you; so, this is Nina.
Nina stood up. "I didn't know what to do. I have a friend who says she is, "a bit of a potter". I asked her for a couple of unfinished work for me to work on. She reached down and put her canvas bag on the table; so, she gave me these three vases; and

this is what I did. The first one was the dancer and she told them it was her favorite, the next one was what she called her ex-libris design and the last was the decanter of red wine." She passed them on and waited.
Andy first reached out for the dancer, rotated it in his hands and then passed it on. He took the ex-libris design and studied it for a long time, at last he held the decanter and studied the wine inside from all angles.
He waited too.
There were seven others there, the vases were passed from one to the other until everyone had a look. The group turned to Lance, the oldest member.
"I think the artwork is just fine. The form of the dancer is implicit in the fine lines of the figure: the body lines, the form of the motions, the touching of the hands, the reaching out to the ends of her touch; very good, the ex-libris is very good, the reaching out of the emblems to whoever has the book is very fetching; the wine is good, but the shape of the vase is not right. But all in everything – a very creditable showing on one week-ends work." He smiled, "very creditable."
Other members had their say, but it was Lance's that stuck in her mind.
Then Lance summed up his views.

"Your skill is in the single stroke work you do well. Picasso, Matisse, Derain and others you do it without apology and you do it well."
But Nina said. "But I don't want to do just that; I was looking for someone to tutor me in lots of colors, oil paintings and other stuff I have not even heard of. That's why I came here; to find out about those things."
"Well," Lance smiled, "I could help you with oil paintings, that's most of my work,
You could come to my studio a couple of mornings a week, we can explore oil paint together, it has been a long time since I had student, would you like that," he studied her filling form, "just until the baby is born; then you can decide to do some work in water color, or acrylic or whatever you think?"
He smiled, a helpful smile from an artist, Nina thought of it.
"That's a very generous offer," Nina said, "very generous, I thank you. What days and time will I start next week?"
The meeting went on to the topics that would have been discussed and Nina listened and then departed silently as topics ranged in the subjects they were familiar with.
She hurried home for cheese, wine, home-made bread and Ouzo dinner with lots to tell Sam about her plans.

They luxuriated in the Sam meal, Sam listened carefully and was very pleased at the apprenticeship with Lance and predicted she would be kept busy until she had another mouth to look after.

Then Nina opened a subject that had been in her mind for a few days now.

"You know you told me about Val selling her slip, and she thought to find a place more suited to bringing up a child? I don't know how well you knew her, but she works for you and Arnold and all that. Could you not offer her a place by Leila on our dock until she finds a place to be permanent?"

"Yes, I did think about it; I wasn't sure what you would think, I didn't know when it might end, I never was really sure about what the background was for her keeping the baby, young as she is. I never did think about it."

"Are you afraid of me being jealous?" Asked Nina.

"Yes, well, not really, but I never wanted to do anything that caused you to doubt me."

"Why don't you try to help her, might be a good thing for all of us to have another mother around. See what she thinks."

Sam got the local pile driver man to tow his rig up and sink four more piles, two at each end and extend the dock by twelve feet each end, they moved Leila up to end, tied up stern in and had the Tom, the builder friend, come and replace the electrical outlets with two new ones. After Sam finished his day's work, he placed two new water outlets on the dock.

So, in two more weeks they got a phone call that Val would be in tomorrow.

And by mid-morning Nina was out there helping her tie up. Nina waited until Val invited her, Nia was very anxious to see Francis in his sea arrangement. He was hanging in his bouncing toy hanging from a ring in the ceiling. "Hello," he smiled, "mom says we are going to live with you for a while."

"That's nice Francis, we are looking forward to that. When you are settled in you can walk up our garden path and have a cookie with us. She turned to Val, you will come on up to see us, and we have to see the toilet, there is not waste down here."

So, the "new people" settled in; and Francis set about with will walking with the dogs, well, not all the way but each day he pestered until he did. Sam and Nina let Val get on with her life; Sam let her use his old car, Nina used the "newer" one. She started her association with Lance; sometimes standing or sitting while he worked on a painting, sometimes working on her own easel trying techniques she saw him use; she had, from the first, expressed a keen interest in oil painting with a brush and a pallet knife; she leaned more and more to this until Lance gave up and spent six of her visits on this technique. She spent the last four of her visits with Lance doing a hanging-on-the-wall portrait of an old snapshot of Giuirdre; she bought a frame from Lance and used his equipment to make an elegant mat, it was a nice thing and she was going to give it to Sam for all the time she had been away.

"Thank you very much for my little apprenticeship," thanked Nina as she carried her belongings to the door. "I really did learn a lot from you and, well, when my baby comes and is good for a good while might I come back from time to time to work with you and explore some things?"

"Of course," replied Lance, "it will give me pleasure, and my wife can come and get a revisitation of the time when she looked after her own kids."

Nina went home to the house that was now in use: the living rooms, the Victorian bathroom, her cherished room of artistic work, the bedroom, the nursery and the kitchen partly from Giuirdre with the wood stove. She parked the car and walked in. Sam was sitting by the stove with Jess and Tina.

"Back then Nina, and this was the last for a bit."

"Yes, Lance said I could go back when I want to, his wife will want to see the baby as well. I brought you something for all the time and pleasure you have given me over this," and she held up her hands, "I really do understand; so that's why I made this for us."

She gave him the oil portrait and he stood looking at it; then he placed it on the countertop and looked some more.

"It is really how I see her in my mind. Thank you Nina."

Chapter 16. Art and Amalia.

Art is not a handicraft, it is the transmission
of feeling the artist has experienced.

Leo Tolstoy. What is Art.

Her time grew near, Nina was excited, but nothing seemed to change her mind these times; most days she spent a couple of hours in her studio; she was painting increasingly elaborate and complex ceramic designs that Katy produced from her endless ideas of shapes, Katy had decided, for now anyway, to offer her designs, Nina decorated and otherwise, via a gallery that promoted unusual designs from new artists; the thought for a gallery of her own had been put aside for the moment. But also, Nina turned her attention to her own work; she was experimenting with her single stroke art designs but also becoming immersed in oil paintings, especially paintings done by pallet knives and brush work. She often awoke from her painting to an everyday time when something disturbed her and she ran off to make dinner or some other arrangement with Sam.

But she was increasingly constrained by her girth and clumsiness, she would be glad now to leave all that behind and return to her previous self. As the time for her confinement grew near, Sam grew more infectious with his closeness and fussing around her, she understood this and so far, had been able to suffer through it, but the time may come when she needed to be able to run her own route.
Happily, this did not occur because a week or so early she called him from his work room to get her bag and drive her to the hospital.
He drove there, parked and got her admitted, went to park the car and took a book and went back to wait.
He read for a bit, he got a cup of coffee for a bit, he nodded off for a bit and stared into space wondering what it would be like sharing lives; he was sure, very sure he was not going to be any different with Nina than now, although he couldn't really picture how it would be with the three of them, his thoughts ranged. Val said she had bought a house (bought a house!) and asked if she could leave her boat at their dock, at least for a time. He was a little sad that she was going, he and Nina liked having Val and Francis with them - - ah well. The book was not absorbing, nothing would at times like this. He nodded off again for another bit. Then there was a nurse

looking at him with a smile and an invitation. He hurried in and knelt beside the bed.
"Are you all right my love? Are you all right?"
"Yes, I'm fine, all that dog walking I expect; now go over there and look at your daughter, very sweet she is."
He did go but the bundle of infant personality looked like many others that he had seen; because she had no name. So, he got close to her and so Nina could hear and he said very softly.
"Hello Amelia Gwyneth Farston, how are you on this first birthday. How are you?"
In three days, he took her home; Val was still there still packing stuff from the boat to take to her house. So, Sam laughed at her.
"Got a house, got a car of your own, got a baby toddler, got a job with Arnold; my you have rejoined the world Val."
But Val was not interested in his greeting, she wanted to see Amelia. She did and was properly admired, gave her a present and went on with her packing but saying she would be by later to say a goodbye.
"Well, what have you done useful while I was away?" Asked Nina.
"Come and see then," replied Sam, "upstairs, come upstairs."
He led the way up to her studio and opened the door.

"See, look at your studio."
The painting materials were unchanged, but there was a carry-cot in one place on a trestle bed and an infant proper bed in a corner. A table with all the stuff for caring for a baby together with a carry out plastic bag for trash.
"See, everything is here, for looking after Amelia, including a two-way set to my room if you need me for something. Now this is all for you to go on painting on your own, and I called your other artist fellow telling him you would be ready to come and be an apprentice, he said they had already heard of your work with Lance and are looking forward to some more. So, you must go on with your work; I have my job with Arthur, we are doing very well and have hired an office manager and plan to hire another to help her. So, we are all right and this year's profits were finished and we, you and I, have to hundred and eight thousand, about twenty percent more than Arnold predicted."
So, like most first time parents do, they wound their way into their joint venture of living: the meals, the night time crying, the peaceful times when Amelia was asleep and Nina was painting; they grew accustomed to each other and even Amelia became accustomed to spending time reaching for her toes and trying to touch the decorations on her crib. So, Nina's not just a

desire, but the need to work with the next painter came to the fore and, equipped with carry cot and full child care for gear, set out to a new mentor. This painter led the way to Nina's later work: the mixing of paints, the under-color painting for later colors, the use of brushes, not just in the conventional way but in pushing, the use of brushing methods the showing of techniques that could only be known by experience. She used her time there for trying things she learned she did not feel the need to paint a picture until her time there was almost complete. Then she used a background paint and painted a large canvas of Amelia there in the studio, a treasure she had framed and given to Hugh the teacher, who cared for it for a while and in the search for a better home for it, took it into their living room where his wife gave it a place on the wall beside the fireplace.

Nina was invited, and attended, the weekly meetings of the "Fine Arts" people as Sam called them. He was overtly proud of her going there and eager to be a help in whatever painting project she decided to get involved in. But that was it; she didn't know. The other painters talked about work they got involved in and, often, they talked about other painter's work, both famous and known to them. They asked Nina from time to time what she was involved in, but she told them nothing, because that was what it was nothing. She had served a private tutoring, went to their meetings, but had nothing to absorb her. In the end they began to gang up on her.

"What do you want to paint? What interests you? Don't you feel moved to paint something? Isn't there anything that moves you to paint. Is there nothing that makes you pick up a brush?

"I don't know," she replied, "when I was with Lance I did this portrait of the lady who gave us our house and it was OK, when I was with Hugh I did a watercolor of my baby and he has it, and now his wife has it in their living room; but now I don't know what I want to paint. I think of subjects that are of interest to me and I come up blank; a person of interest, someone inspirational, at least to me, a scene of importance, something; but now nothing holds my interest enough for me to paint them."

"Well, what does interest you? There must be something or somebody's, there must be something."

"Well - - you guys are interesting to me, with your quirks and fables about art and artists, there are lots of things within you that could be portrayed."

"Well, there you are then, paint us; and when your work is done, we can all be together to talk about what you saw and how you painted it."

And so it was; the six crucible artist’s artistic evaluation.

Chapter 17.—In an Artist's mind?

What art is mine;
Our state cannot be sevr'd, we are one,
One flesh; to lose thee were to lose myself.
John Milton. *Paradise Lost.*

Nina put her feet up for a rest, her mind was sort of empty, she just thought. Tina found her on the couch and came to get up and rest her head on Nina's knees and offer what help she could, she could snuggle up to her special person and feel happy, she could raise her eyebrows and look at the door and the way to the river bank, she could look up hoping for a hand stroking, all these dog things, but in the end she sighed, laid down her head and went to sleep.

Nina, however, was lost in thought, or she thought it was thought, perhaps it was dreams, about stuff that might have been; or may have been; but now; with Sam and the rest of them, could be real anyway; a real artist. A real artist, she thought, what kind of an artist? She really wasn't much of anything, she thought.

"Really famous artists became famous for their interpretation of things; but no, that's not just true; Henry Moore created large stone images; I don't understand all of them; but most people do, they understand them and value them, they adorn the gardens of lots of buildings which are involved with art; but I'm not like him; I have to decide how I want to express myself, if I can. Well, how am I? She fiddled with Tina's ears and reached into her mind for the art which brought most joy. Henry Moore was an artist all his life, he lived among his contemporaries and he married a young artist. He thought art every waking moment, he said, oh I forget, about his simple lines - - "art should have a certain mystery and should make demands on the spectator"; but he was serious about his work, he made a sculpture that stands outside near the building where Enrico Fermi led the team that produced the first controlled nuclear reaction; and look at it and wonder what it is, some thought it was mushroom cloud topped with a skull, but Moore hoped that visitors would look thought it as if it were a cathedral and they were looking through apertures. I might have thought it was a sort of joke. A sculpture like that, outside that building, but I'm not like him, not at all; what really stirs me up? Well, I confess to myself it's the impressionist paintings from Europe, the 1830's to the 1920's the imagination and diversity that's what stirs me up; Paul Gauguin, a cherished artist now, but unappreciated in France during his life, but his images of native women brings tears to my eyes; and all the others, they were experimenters, that's what they were, color experimenters and most of them went about art in a way that made them not a part of someone else's life, or so it seemed to me.

But I can't do that; I have to be a part of other things; my life with Sam the children? And others, I have to be part of a society, and what about the others: Claude Monet and the Garden at Giverny – that's more like me, the colors and the feelings of the flowers, and Pierre August Renoir- all those scenes with people, and Matisse and his dancers full of life, Degas with his movement and his night scene of the Absinthe Drinker - - oh! What wonderful people to live among.

But nowadays, we don't seem to pay much attention to artists, we are more interested in computer game designers; is that where our talent goes these times? What if Amelia Gwyneth Farston grew into artistic thoughts; what would we do then? Nothing, that's what we will do, encourage her to follow her interests, that's what we will do. But we're lucky, she can do whatever she wants, because of us – her parents, so what will I do? That's what I'm thinking of, what will I do?

.

Chapter 18—Artistic Adroitness.

Life is the art of drawing sufficient conclusions from insufficient premises
Samuel Butler *Note Books. Life,*

Nina went about her new artist endeavor with a new fever; she chose for her first of the six subjects, one who she didn't know as well as Lance and Hugh, but well enough to bring a sense of what she thought would be realism to her grasp of his character.

She set out with Amelia for a coffee meeting with Randolph, her first subject. She asked about how he wanted to be an artist and how it brought him here. She asked after his parents, what they did and how they thought of his career; she asked how he spent his time during his growing up and she enquired why he was called Randolph. She got his wife to come in and talk about their time together before they married; and later one of the younger children came home from school and she joined in too. On her second meeting she took about twenty copies of paintings that she liked and disliked, she sat with him while he talked about the work and how he saw it. He spoke about the place and time in history when the work was painted, and what if that had any influence on the work.

When that was over, she asked him how he should be portrayed in materials, paper, color and texture. Then she took her camera and took about twelve pictures of him to study for her arrangement. Finally, she let him go with a heartfelt thank you and together with her new 'understandings' she went home with Amelia to ponder her work with Randolph.

She lay back in her studio armchair and thought about Randolph; an image began to emerge.

"I see him in a not misty but slightly unclear person, not behind all that's happening, but still all directing things from there, I see him as loving to family and friends and appreciative of his growing up life. I see him in oils with brushes to make him fit my view of him. He is nice to be with, pleasant to talk to, his views are something in line with what I think, he is I think, flexible in his outlook but not beyond a certain point."

She gathered these notes on an index card and took them with Amelia, her paints, easel and a canvas to her first sitting, accompanied by Amelia. She told Randolph about her 'survey' of his characteristics and temperament, told him his canvas would be in oils with brush marks and got him to sit on a high stool in his normal work clothes.

Although it was to be in oils, she outlined the figure and the stool in Conté stick and stood back to see how that suited her ideas. She began to lay in colors with a pallet knife and brush them into shape. There came a time when she was tired and progress had been made.

"So, we'll let this ride until the next sitting. And when can that be?"

Randolph gave her a couple of hours the day after tomorrow and she was happy with that. She went in with Amelia to say hello to Trina, Randolph's wife and then off home to Sam and the dogs. The next sitting Nina filled in more colors and more unclear detail, took a few more photos and said, "that's all, Randolph, I'll see you when I am finished."

She worked on it, on and off for a couple more weeks and got a frame for it and showed Sam.

"This is my first portrait of my peers. This is the list I made of the things I could see in him; I did attach a couple more as I went along. This is the portrait I made and I think, I tried, to embody all the things I saw of him."

And she took the cover off and let Sam see it.

He looked at it for a while.

"Well, I don't know the man nor what he looks like. But I see in the image a lot of what you have on your index card, but I have not any knowledge to bring to bear. I'm sorry, you'll have to show it to your peers and see what they think."

With Amelia at the next meeting of her peers she took the painting in a cover and six copies of her index card, with a couple of additions as she painted, to give to the group. The meeting looked at her with expectation so she began.

"This is the first portrait for your evaluation. I did something to begin, something that would normally grow in your mind as you proceeded to paint; I think, but this time I wondered where it might lead me; I show it to you that you will know how I understood the subject and where I thought the image would grow into; so this is my index card of where I wanted the portrait of Randolph would be."

She gave each member a copy of her index card for them to read.

Then she got up and walked to the end of the table and unwrapped the framed painting and rested it on the table for them to inspect.

"This is my painting of Randolph for you to talk about. I can't tell you all that was in my mind as I painted, but I thought about Randolph's growing up, the childhood friends he had, going to art school, meeting Trina and beginning married life, the children and where he found himself in artists and among artists like you.

I'm going to offer it to Tina, if she will have it and if Randolph will permit it."

They pursued their talk of the picture, Randolph said much of his past seemed present; but Nina did not gain anything from the conversations, no suggested avenues that could have been explored, no personal prejudices that was touched on; she selected to accept their comments and then asked Trina to come in to see it. She came in and looked at the painting. Looked at it for a long quiet time; then turned to Nina and told her it was a wonderful painting and a super gift; she would hang it in her living room where all who came would see it.

She went on with her painting, the rest of her group and with another two visits with two other painters. Then, quite by accident, she realized that was what her personal artistic adroitness and artifices were: personalities, the real and hidden persona; she would concentrate on portraits.

It was a moment of truth that she had begun to think was missing from her mind, but now she was sure it was there.

When she went to the next meeting with her group, she told them of the realization, they just nodded and pressed on; they knew this a while ago.

But, all of that was a part of her life; other parts existed, maybe more important parts; she had to consider them; Amelia was six months old,

growing bigger, what was next? She would have to discuss the future with Sam.
One evening, the next good evening in Giuirdre's kitchen, replete with a fish stew and a glass or two of white wine, she approached her decision, that Sam is to help her with. She told him she had a decision to take, with her life, and she wanted him to help her.
"I have realized that my artistic scent, the thing that makes me able to give; is that I think I can see people inside and paint those characteristics in a painting, I think I'm good at that and that's my offer towards my art. I'm comfortable with it. When I go with Amelia, we are happy, she lies in her cot and then we get her out for a change, a nappy, some food or just to be together for a bit. I can imagine how things will change as she grows up; can move around, can walk, can play on her own, can begin to amuse herself; I can imagine that and understand it. So, Amelia and I, we can look forward to a life together and then as she starts school, we can see it blended together with the other part of our lives.
That is very good for me and my art and for Amelia who will have interested company for as long as she wants it.
However, now, is the time when I thought we could begin a second baby; and I had begun to make the necessary plans for that. But now I think

the life I have in mind for Amelia and I would be changed, forever, never to be like this. My art has become very important to me, life with Amelia is the same, now I'm planning to change all that - - - forever. I don't know what to make of this Sam. Do you have any views?"

"That's hard. That's very hard; we have always thought of having two children, you were the originator of that as much as me, but now your art has become another central part of your life, a real force within you and now you have this precedent to deal with. Well, let me think about that for a day or two, will you let me do that?"

Sam lay awake that night thinking about Nina's difficulty. He has realized that her new belief in her art has become important to her, and he feels that it is important to him also, he wants her to be content in all that. But he is worried about her considering trying to have the children but giving up her art world to make it work. He could, at the end of several sleepless hours, only have one answer. And to see if this answer works, he would have to visit Arnold tomorrow.

After breakfast he told Nina he needed to go in to visit Arnold. When he got there Arnold said.

"Another meeting? You always come in at the end of the week."

"No, not another meeting, this is quite different, way different. You sometimes complain about

your elder sister who lives in the little apartment at the end of your barn. Is she still there?"
"Yes, still there. Likely to be there forever."
"Tell me a bit more about her."
"She was married, trying for a long time to have a baby. Then her husband, who was quite a bit older, died of a stroke or a heart attack or something. He was a partner in a good real estate company; the other half bought out from Cassie and she came here in my vacant apartment for a spell, three years ago. My apartment is not rented like it should and she has no skills for getting a job nor any desire to move along."
"Let me explain why I asked. Sam said if he got a small apartment built on his house and he and Nina could offer Cassie a job helping to look after their kids, and one not born yet, did Arnold think that would work? And Cassie, how might she think of that?"
Arnold thought Cassie might like job looking after children, might make the best of her, and Sam should ask her.
Sam said he would, but after talking to Nina. He thanked Arnold and went back to see Nina.
Up in her studio Nina was despondent, she couldn't find any answer to her trial. The best solution was to reign in her art work until the two children were old enough to release her to spend the time she felt was needed.

But when Sam came home, he came upstairs to meet her he had that glint in his eyes that she had seen times before.
“Hello,” Sam said, “you have time to talk to me? Of course, Sam, of course.”
“Here is on suggestion for you to consider. It is for you to consider first; I have taken no action as yet. I thought a long time about this last night; I didn’t want you to not continue with your art work. I hated the idea of that. I hated the idea of you not having two children, I hated that too. I began to think about what it would take to do both. And that was to have a second child and go on as you are now, taking one of the children with you and the other child the next time. So, how can that be? Well, we need a person, a real and proper person to live here, in a small apartment I can have built attached to the main house and, where might such a person be? Well, Arnold has an older sister who was widowed several years ago at time when she was trying, unsuccessfully to become pregnant. She came to be “temporarily” in a flat attached to his barn, still here now. Arnold thinks that such a proposition would be very attractive to her: two children to look after, be a part of a family, a place of her own. But, neither of us have spoken to her, I have never even met her.

Now this would leave you free to devote, well, six hours a day to painting with one child for company with the other child happy with a nanny.
So, you think about I and we three with Amelia could go and talk to her, or you could go alone, I could go alone to talk about the apartment, whatever you think.
So, I said I would think about it and that is what my first thought is."
At dinner time Nina said.
"If Arnold suggests it would be all right then all three of us could go and see her, make a suggestion, ask her to come out here, explain that it will not be for a while as I am not pregnant yet, and anyway, there will be time to build the apartment. If we all feel OK to carry on then we can make some plans.
And - - - - I feel valued and treasured by you for thinking the way you do. Thank you. And, as you have made it possible to continue, when bed time comes we can made some attempt to put all this into motion, even if what's her name ' chassie' isn't interested, we could fine someone else or even au pair or something."
But following intervention by Arnold, the three of them went in a couple of days' time to visit Chassie. Sam took note of the condition of her apartment and Nina paid attention to her attention she paid Amelia.

Sam told Chassie all about their situation. He told her he would get a small apartment built and they were looking for someone who would help look after two children, although they only had one at the moment. He thought this would all come together in about nine months and anyway, they were going to build the apartment. They thought she could think about it and perhaps come out and visit the house and see what it was like. He knew this was all new to her so it would be up to her to give a call and come out, if she was interested."

Well, she did come out and played with Amelia, spent time with Nina. Nina liked her and they agreed that an initial arrangement of say six months of trial would be good and it would start when the apartment was finished.

Three weeks later Nina had another yellow plastic holder to show Sam and the arrangement was in place.

Chapter 19.—The hospital Again.

If any thing delight me for to print
My book, tis this; that Thou, my God art in't
Robert Herrick. The Virgin Mary.

Another drive to the hospital, another admitting another waiting and another father's voice over the bed clothes.
"Hello, Alexis Gelene, how are you today on your first birthday, OK?"
Amelia was at home with Cassie; the change in the family happened earlier than the original plan; Tom the builder was anxious to work on a very compact apartment and plans were drawn and approved and now there was a studio apartment at the north end of the house. Cassie's increasing anxiousness added to the schedule, her dream of escaping from Arnold's barn added to her burning desire to be involved in the upbringing of two children burned brightly in the changes to their lives. So, she was there and the danger of filtering off their child's affection and love to another "parent" was something that Nina and Sam realized but stood back and waited in ambush to deal with it when it came.
But now a new life began with Alexis and changes in all things.

Sam and Arnold had begun a new phase in their business; partly due to a 'keep improving or die' in their business world and partly to free up more of their personal lives for personal family pleasures; so, after some head-scratching in their weekly meetings, they agreed to "promote' Val from being a software contributor to Program Management over the two young girls who had been evaluating new and revised work. Val's wider role would be to channel the work of those girls to a company niche but also to work towards building the niche into, something that they didn't know – that was her job and Arnold and Sam would help her figure that out and soon it would be part of the weekly meeting too.

Cassie's work schedule was pretty much what she wanted; which was to be with at least one of the children. So, she came for breakfast, stayed most of the morning and went home for a very long lunch and back again to take one or other for a walk and stay for their dinner time. Sometimes she would stay and give one or the other a bath. She was happy to do anything with the babies.

Sam was, with Arnold, trying to reduce the time spent in work; Sam was having fun-on-the-dock with the boat; he had a full length Sunbrella cover made for the whole boat, so in the spring, summer and fall it was covered from the sun; now he waxed and polished all the white work and

spent a long time putting new gel coat everywhere; the boat looked very good and well loved, later in the winter months he had a number of upgrades and changes to make below.
Nina slowly turned back into her art work; but slowly. First, she had to do something about the nine months of getting ready, she got Sam to join her in a daily visit to the gym. They would go out five thirty and work out until seven; Nina joined Pilates classes and a yogurt class and did elliptical exercises in the other times; they both felt better and said they would never stop now.
But in her art work she still went to her weekly meeting with the group, but these days she was a tried and true member and not an ad-hoc member.
But for work she had no planned, no work planned. She did some new pots for Kathy, pots and other vases that she began to color with bright and sometimes very faded colors, these new designs proved very popular, but this work didn't satisfy her very much, she needed some work like the portraits she did for her group, but nothing seemed to surface for her.
One lunchtime Sam came in with a smile.
"I got a call that one of our old sailing friends came home; about the time when I bought our boat he sailed off for some time alone, or so he said, but it turns out he sailed around the world,

in a leisurely way, stopping where he liked and or where he could get work for a while; well he's back and a little get together is planned for next Saturday, will you come with me please, I would like you to meet him.
On Saturday Cassie was very happy to be left in sole charge of the babies and they went off to the humble sailing club that Sam used to belong to. Gregg, the sailor, was surrounded by old friends and Sam and Nina had to wait a bit to meet him. He was a washed version of his sailing persona; old jeans, soft flannel shirt, boat shoes with no socks, sun-browned face, very long hair with an unusual tie back. All this Nina could see as she waited with Sam to say 'hello'. When they did get there Sam greeted him with news of the others and introduced Nina, who shook his hand and said, before letting his hand go.
"Come and visit us, be prepared to have your portrait painted and come dressed as you are now - - promise!"
And she melted away with Sam, to meet lots of other old friends and then to go home.
In a few days Sam told her that Gregg was coming for a visit.
When he did come, they had lunch and Gregg told them about his trip.
"Not a trip at all," he said, "just a five-year long-term visit to places and people I would never have

otherwise seen. Lots of people to listen to, lots of things to say, lots to learn if you pay attention; so, part way around I started to make notes and further on this developed into an essay and then a book, and that's where it is now; I have a publisher interested but he wants some art work and that is my next venture, see how that can be done."

Nina said, "come over here, this is a portrait I painted of the lady who gave us this house,"

And here, she said, "are copies of the paintings I did for my art group. Now what I suggest is for you to have me paint a portrait of you for you to use in your book, I could do chapter headings, groups to illustrate scenes from photos you have, the cover of your book to your personal specification and all here by the water with your old friend, Sam. What do you think? Begin with a portrait of you and if you don't like it then it's free; what do you think? Start tomorrow, begin by discussing the type of image that you have in mind.

Now, a couple of things, I want to hold the property rights for the work I do, and, I want my name on the title page below your name with mine as illustrator - - all right?"

And so, her art work began, again. Next day, with Gregg dressed like Nia wanted and they discussed the portrait of Gregg; Nina could see that her pallet and brush technique was not suitable; they discussed the image of Gregg and they talked about the cover of the book, chapter title illustrations, the back cover of the book and Gregg would go away and count the number of illustrations that could be in the based on the photographs he had.

Nina got out art books and they discussed the portrait, how he imagined it in his mind; they looked at portraits old and more recent, but Gregg did not have a strong view, so she said she would go ahead and see what they thought. They thought of him holding the wheel or other nautical poses, but they both agreed it was not what they thought of, so it would be a three-quarter height portrait.

So, the portrait of Gregg began, it was a softer, more intimate image than was her previous works but as things progressed, she began to like it more and more. Then she began to get tired and called a halt for that day. Gregg said he would be back tomorrow, and Nina had time to play some simple hand waving games with Amelia.

Sam was off on his child caring trips too; he had somehow developed a private feeling with baby Alexis, from the time he first met her in the hospital. So, with Jess, he took Alexis in her body baby carrier, he got her settled in on his chest with a half-way bottle keeping warm, made sure he had his phone with him and set off with Jess for a walk along the river bank. He walked in relaxation, his thoughts drawn with the way his life had progressed and with the girlish baby in his arms, what she would be, what things she must do whether she had art streaks in her being like her mother.

He was most happy with the way Nina's life had developed, happy that she had something special for her; pleased too that with Arnold they are building their business up into the niche structure they wanted; all real work and no frills; glad they had promoted Val to be office manager and he thought they could, Arnold and Sam, give up say five percent of ownership and make Val a director, he thought he could bring that up with Arnold very soon.

Now Sam was at the half way point and he sat on the log and got out the bottle for Alexis. He held her gently and watched her drink her bottle, then give a burb and snuggle in her warm world for the walk back home again. On the way home he thought of tomorrow and Nina's work on Gregg's portrait and the further work on the illustrations for the book; he was content for all that in her future.

The following morning Nina and Gregg worked on his portrait again, Nina reached a point where she wanted to go on her own for a while, and they turned their thoughts to the illustrations that preceded each chapter and the in-chapter illustrations of the events in the book. Gregg said he would collect all his photos and organize them on a USB disc and they could jointly study them and begin to create them into things Nina could use; Gregg said he would be back next week after Nina had done most of the portrait work.

Thus, Nina and Gregg together moved on with the art work for his book. The portrait pleased Gregg so much that he decided to use it for the cover of his book and so Nina painted another for the interior of the book, this time she let her own interests take charge and this one was a pallet and oil version, and strangely, that caught Gregg's eye as well.

When Nina was finished, she had prepared art work so that each chapter was preceded by an illustration painted from photos that Gregg had taken, scenes from his adventures, people he had met, the special places he visited. And twice through each chapter there was a full-size portrayal of another milestone in his trip. Finally, it was all together; Gregg assembled everything in a folder of text, the covers and a separate folder of the art work for any extra work.

They sat with Sam and had a long dinner and talk and waited for the publisher to provide their comments.

In about four weeks Gregg had an appointment with the publisher; he called Nina to ask what he should wear; she told him to wear what he had on for the portrait he had chosen for the cover of the book. So, he did.

At the meeting he was met by the editor of the outdoor lives' publications. He was very complimentary about the book; the movement from one chapter to the next, progressing along his path around the world, the choice of the interviews and meetings with the people he met, and, of course, the illustrations that brought out the story and allowed the reader to meet the people and the story.

They were going to publish it with just a review, all the artwork was going to be used and the folder of artwork would be used to create a little bookstore within a bookstore to be a separate place to show the book. They wanted him to have a limited book signing and they wanted the illustrator to come for a few of these. Gregg went home and then to see Nina about her attendances with him.

Gregg went off on his book signing and Nina went on two just to please him. Nina was more excited about what, she hoped, would come next.

Chapter 20.—Books Again.

A good book is the best of friends,
The same to-day and for ever.
Martin Farquhar Tupper Proverbial Philosophy.

She did not have very long to wait. A few weeks after her second
Gregg-book-review, she received a call from Gregg's publisher asking if she would consider doing cover and/or illustrations for a new book that they were contemplating, would she call and learn all about the project?
She did and learned that the book was written by a retired policeman, writing about some of the crimes he had been involved in, she studied the suggested art list and told them she was not interested in the work. She then carried on with some personal projects while she wondered about her future.
Later, she received a call from someone who had seen one of the "miniature bookstores" selling Gregg's book. She looked at the artwork and bought one of Gregg's books and fell in love with all the artwork. The author asked if she could come for a visit and Nina said she could. The next day, soon after breakfast, a knock came at the

door and Nina, Amelia and Alexis went to open it. The lady author was there with a faded and scratched portfolio and a smiling face with half-moon glasses.
“Good morning family,” she greeted them, “I’ve come to see about art work for my book.”
She got a variable family response, Nina said hello, Amelia said Tina had had a very big scratch on her ear and Alex gave her a big smile. Nina invited her into the kitchen.
“You’ll have to wait a bit, Cassie, who looks after the children will be here in a moment; would you like a cup of coffee while we wait?”
Thy each had their coffee and Hilary, the lady’s name, talked about having children; Hilary had two also, one at work as a vet and the other off on some adventure with two other girls wandering in New Zealand.
“A blessed thing when they get that old; but not really for me, I loved them around and now there’s me, the cat Woodbine and my dog April because he came in April. He’s patiently waiting for me in the car.”
“Can’t you bring April in here?” Asked Nina.
“Oh, sure, he’ll be delighted and kiss everyone several times, but if you don’t mind, he will feel a part of things.”
So off she went for April and came back with a bright dog about the size of Tina but April had an

interesting facemask of black and white curly hairs.

But then Cassie came in then and so Nina, Hilary April and Tina went up to her studio to talk about Hilary's art work.

I have written a book for children about eight or ten years old; a bit too much for toddlers but not so much. The book is direct challenge to smart phones and whatever else there may be to "occupy" small children. The editor is a woman and I suspect my book fills the place of some hostage that each editor has once in a while to show - - - well, something. So, it is a book that tells a story that can be read, by the child or by a grownup, but is enriched by the artwork that is an integral part of the tale. In fact, the artwork will make or break the story; and that's why I want to talk to you.

Here is a copy of the text, arranged in a way that I would have it as a book, it could be revised or expanded to suit the illustrations or to meet some changes. But here is the story and it needs some illustrations like you did for Gregg's book.

Nina looked through the book.

"I don't know if the illustrations that I choose would be the ones that you might have in mind."

"Can you make a few sketches of some and we see how we each see them, or not?"

"Leave it with me, I'll call you and we can get together."

But Nina had throughout this discussion, been thinking about a better way. She called Katy.

"She asked if she could borrow her daughters that afternoon, she said she wanted them to help her and Katy could tell them that she would pay them and what about that?"

Nina made two copies of Hilary's text and got a couple of plain folders of sketch paper, said goodbye to the girls, Jess and Tina, gave a goodbye kiss to Sam and told him she was off to Katy."

When she got there she told Amy and Case that she had a book to make illustration for, but she didn't know what the illustrations should be and she wanted their help.

She also told them she would pay for their help, so what about helping, would they help her?

They unanimously agreed and were ready to start.

She sat them at a table, one each side of her, opened the book and showed them a couple of pages.

"I will read you the story and when we come to a place where a picture comes in, you will tell me what the picture should be. OK?"

She began to read the story; when, two pages on there was a place.

"So, what picture would fit in here?"

The girls talked about it and eventually agreed. So, Nina took her scrap pad and drew an outline of the picture they described. They told her what was wrong and she drew another; this on was better so Nina added clothes and some expressions; the girls said it was OK and Nina read on until the next place. This went on for a couple of hours and Nina could tell the girls were tiring.

"She said it was all good and could she come back tomorrow to go on? And, should she pay them now or a big payment at the end? They chose the big payment.

Between then and tomorrow Nina painted preliminary color pictures in the draft pages of the book to show them to the girls and get final comments.

Tomorrow the girls looked over the colored pictures and offered comments that Nina recorded in a note book.

This process went on for six days until Nina had all the children's comments, and colored pictures in her draft book.

Then she got Katy in and Nina told the girls.

"You worked for six days on this book. Two hours a day is twelve hours. Twelve hours at five dollars an hour is Sixty dollars, but you did very well with your work so this is a hundred dollars for you each. And 'Thank You' very much."

The girls were delighted but turned to Katy to see what they could spend it on. Katy did not reply. But Katy did give Nina an affectionate hug.

So now Nina had a book full of little girls' visions. Some were like she would have chosen on her own; some were very different but still, in the misty darkness of understanding she could see them; but about a quarter of the pictures were beyond her reach. But still, she called Hillary to come and see.

When she came Nina told her how she got two small friends to define the pictures; She did not edit what they told her; she said there was a four-step process to get the pictures that they saw. And anyway; here is your book.

Hillary ran through her pages and then sat back and did it carefully and thoughtfully; this took a couple of hours so Nina sat and read, and waited.

Eventually she sat up and said,

"I don't know, I just don't know about this. I shall have to take it with me. Although I understand that I might have a bomb in my hands."

Two weeks passed by, Nina waited for Hillary, she came one afternoon, bringing her book.

"When I left here with the book, I was almost sure I wasn't going to use it; but; I did take to a friend who is, or was, a children's teacher. She read the book and laughed out loud at some of the parts of it, she was sure that children would too, except some of the "far out" characters and speech were beyond her, but she suggested another get together with a child psychologist, so we both went to see her and she recognized some, but not all, of the children's stuff. She said if it were her book, she would publish it, some parents might have something to say, but you could always refer them to the originators who, she smiled as she said this, "Could explain it." But it was not her book and that was her advice."

"That was where my research took me; so, I am here to ask something. I had planned to list your name under my name as the book illustrator, could it be that I could also list your assistant's names as Illustrator Advisors?"

Nina laughed at that.

"Well, I will drive over to Katy's and ask her and ask the girls. But I see nothing wrong with that, I think how proud I would be if they were my daughters."

She left the girls with Cassie and hurried off to see Katy. She explained the book and the little conundrum or illusion this might show if the author and the publisher could not explain some of the words, so a solution suggested was that my name will go beneath the authors and below that would be Amy and Case who would be "Illustrator's Advisors", I thought I would come and see what you thought of it and, if you liked it, we could ask your girls."

Everybody liked it, especially Amy and Case who would have their name in a book.

Of went Hillary to get her book published and that was the end of the story, or not.

Nina received small rewards from the sale of Gregg's book on his tour of the world, small amounts but steady, indicating that his book had a small but perhaps growing group of people who still read that sort of thing. But in about three months' time larger, much larger rewards came from the sale of Hillary's children's book; and it went on, month after month. So, Nina who didn't place much emphasis on these rewards decided to make a monthly submittal to Amy and Case. She made out two checks and drove over to Katy's house and sat with Katy while she explained the source of the money. Katy agreed that Nina would share the proceeds whenever they came; so, Nina could talk to the girls about it. Of course, they were delighted to get a freefall of money, but they were more excited about where it came from. The rewards got shared out and the girls were proud of their share. A bit later Hillary won second prize in a Nationwide competition for children's book, so the rewards became greater for a while.

Then one day, out of the blue, Hillary came to Nina's house for "a visit". She told Nina about her success as a writer and outlined another book. Then she asked Nina for the address of Amy and Case to see about another text.

“No, not from me,” said Nina, “not from me, if you want to get their help you should ask their mother, not me. If that was the reason for your visit here, I’ll get you their address and you can see their mother.”

She filled out a note pad with the address and gave it to her. When she had left Nina called Katy and told her what she had done; she left it to Katy to decide.

Nina went on with her publication work, doing two or three a year, mixed in with her own work which made up her repertoire.

Chapter 21.—Val's Promotion

He that will not apply new remedies must expect
New evils; for time is the greatest innovator.
Francis Bacon. Of Innovations.

Their lives had become a tribal life; Nina had her art work and many friends within that. She had Cassie who was now really a member of the family and with whom she shared the love and responsibility of looking after the children. Amelia and Alexis were growing up into children that were nice to spend time with. Sam had spent two winters working on the interior of their boat, hoping to spend time soon cruising with his family, but this seemed so far away at the moment, nevertheless, the boat formed a place of solitude and a place to be alone with his work in the software business. He had been sharing the development of the company with Arnold; they both felt the company couldn't stay still and survive the way it was; Sam's solution to this was a bit broader than Arnold's, and he had a way to cause a change to help things along, Arnold was not against Sam's idea, but was uncertain of where it might end; but in the end Sam found a way to make it happen to Arnold's satisfaction. So, during one of their weekly meetings, which had included Val for some time, he brought up a new subject.

"Val, Arnold and I have been wondering for some time how to make the company more secure and staying in our place in our niche of work. You are central to our plan and to make things as equal as can be, we have each given up seven and a half percent of our directorship to give to you and to offer you a place on the Board of Governors; with the fifteen percent share. You will join us to help keep our place in our little world. We three have different roles in shaping this future; yours will be, as always, to be aware of and on top of, new business opportunities.

In the past I bought from Arnold my share of the company, he got fifty five percent, I got forty five percent. The arrangement is that if I ever want to leave my directorship, he will pay me back at the price I paid at that time. We don't want you to pay for your share, but if you leave, then the directorship remains here. But the director's share of profits will be yours from now on, and based on last year's and this year's, so far; it will be around sixty thousand, on top of the salary you now earn. We hope this will ensure you and Francis will stay around for a long time."

Val was astonished

"I never thought you think that of me, what a surprise! I had no plans to leave and take Francis anywhere else and now, well, I never even want to think of it."

And so, the company moved into a refreshed and a more integrated way of managing their work. Val was no doubt influenced by her new position; having director's fees like a windfall in her life. Sam had never known about her life before he met her at the marina: a lovely woman, with a four month old baby, alone in her boat and no tale to tell how she got there; and now, intimately involved with her business , still never talking about her life; but, having reached the position Arnold and Sam had offered her, never no need to look back, only to look forward.

Arnold, founder of the business and well content for it to carry on in the form that his joint plan with Sam had been doing well and new work in their field was coming quietly.

And Sam, pretty much like Arnold; they both had financial resources behind them, no need to fear the future, just like to make a success of their lives.

Their company structure was all-important to their success; no offices to look after, no utilities to pay for, Chartered Accountant examined their work and payments each week.

The employees were all remote, the employees that had been retained, by past performance and reliability, were joined to the company by their own needs; a housewife who wrote code in the night when her children were asleep, a man with both legs damaged from a motorcycle accident, could earn a decent salary at home looking out onto his lawn, another youngish woman looking after her aged mother, found lots of time for work, quite a few teenage computer "hackers?" who worked far into the night, and there were others, unknown people, who were important to their software regime. But all these "employees" were a part of their own personal group, the wife of a worker, the son of a working father, a person on unemployment and so, as far as Arnold knew, they had access to health insurance from elsewhere, certainly Arnold could not offer those kind of benefits in the health insurance world that prevailed. So, what was left for Arnold to offer employees to secure their feelings about working for him? He invited his accountant to stay and have a drink after their meeting and Arnold asked him if he could create some kind of investment program that could be used as a "401k package" that could handle employees that come and go or some that work not all the time. He did; and Arnold's workers can now be a part of this program as long as they work, if they take time off, they can pick up again when they get back. Arnold donates one percent of their weekly earnings, and the workers could invest what they could. The scheme was enthusiastically welcomed by the workers and the accountant keeps an eye on things, changing investments and other management strategies.

So, Arnold, Sam and now Val had their world held together by this rag-taggle group of workers with not much to bind them together. This was something that Arnold thought of a lot; but he had run this company for, what was it now - twenty one years; and it only became stronger but around a half of the workers had been with him for most of the time. He pondered this, sometimes, and a couple of times he explored these people's thoughts; but mostly all he got back from them was.

"Leave me alone, you send me work and I do it, that's what I like about it."

He decided that was that, leave them alone and be thankful. Each year he increased the hourly pay and got thanks back from some of them, but the work was done and everybody was happy.

Chapter 22.-Sam's trip backward

All the trees they are so high,
The leaves they are so green,
The day is past and gone, sweetheart.
The Oxford Book of Ballads. The Trees are so High.

Sam gazed into his glass of Malbec but seeing a glimpse of far beyond. Nina waited for him to say something, for this was his way of talking to her of something new or different. Finally, he took another sip and said to her.
"This wine is very good; I think I shall get a case next time I go in."
"Yes, dear, good idea."
"You know Nina, we should go away, for a trip, or preferably on the boat. I think the girls would love that."
"They will; but not yet my love. They are too young for a trip like that. It would be different if we were planning a life for them and us on the boat, that would be different; but we are not. Your trouble is that you have fallen now into a patch of your life where you don't have much to distract you, nothing demanding your attention. We are all coming along nicely, and you just have to join in. The girls are doing well and growing up

nicely; Cassie shows them how to behave, she is helping them to read and do real puzzles, she has them join in when she cooks, and she shows them how to behave even when they would do other things; and the girls come up to my studio and they draw on their tables that you got for them; you take them on little hikes with Jess and they're learning the names of birds and animals; I like the way we are; it will not last, but while it is this way I want it to continue. Family adventures will come, but not just now. But, I have an alternate little plan for you, to be a light relief for your troubled brain: why don't you take Jess and your car and have a week away from work and go and visit the marina you made and all the friends that are still there?"

Sam pondered.

"OK, I think I will do that."

He told Arnold and Val he would be away for a week or so, and next Saturday he packed a canvas hold all, told Jess to be ready for a trip, said he would leave about three in the morning, kissed everybody and went to bed. When his alarm went off he went for Jess and took him and his breakfast to the car and went on his way.

He headed for the Tappan Zee bridge and chose a country route across Pennsylvania, if there are any country routes left to find. But he did choose a modest traffic route and he and Jess went on together, Sam singing to a Beatles anthology and Jess sleeping on the passenger's seat in his travel harness. They had some comfort stops but Sam wanted to get south of Norfolk before they stopped, to be able to get to the marina next morning. They went on country roads and then Sam saw a quiet old-fashioned motel. He pulled in and stopped. There was a man, a younger man, in the office. Sam asked if he could have Jess in his room.

"He has his own bed." He told him.

"No, no way." Said the man.

"OK." Said Sam, preparing to leave.

"No, it's OK." Said the man, "take care then, won't you."

Sam went to his room, nice and cool, simple furniture, good bathroom.

Sam attached a lead to Jess and they went for a walk. Then when they came back Sam took a small cooler from the room and walked to the office.

"My names Sam, this is Jess. We have some beer here, wondered if you could share it with us."

The man looked at them. He smiled.

"My names Dave, love to share with you."

Sam sat down with Jess at his feet, he motioned Jess to be content and lie down, he opened the cooler and offered Guinness or Newcastle Brown ale. Dave took a Guinness and Sam took the ale. Sam said.

"You don't seem to look like a motel manager."
"No, I own it, funny business, my uncle built it and ran it for fifty-five years, then he wanted to move away. I had just retired from the Army and he said he would give it to me."
"Be good experience for me", he said, " the people stopping by here are different; they don't want to be a part of the Holiday Inn / Hilton experience, you'll see; keep it decent, keep the client's content; you'll have a happy time."
"And he was right; all kinds of people stop here, many repeat customers."
He laughed.
"A few young and not so young ladies stop for a couple of days of relaxation away from whatever fills their lives elsewhere; people like you, a drifting off on a little journey, I change the beds, a lady comes and takes them to the laundry, her sister comes and cleans the rooms that were occupied, I sit here and see the world go by; and; say a prayer a day for my far-seeing uncle."
"You retired from the army?"
"Yes, I did. Took a philosophy degree and right after graduation signed up for the Army; twenty years I did. Looking back, it wasn't a bad deal, wasn't for me, anyway, because I'm here now, unlike many of my comrades. Twenty years I did; most all of it fighting in the middle east, what a waste of, well, something."

His mind seemed to drift away, then he said.
"I never knew what to make of it, you know; fighting, fighting for something."
He said.
"What do you think Sam? What do you think? What did you think? You know in philosophy thoughts you think about the ethics of what you do. So, what were the ethics of what we did, what we are doing out there? How about history? The British came to subdue us but we sent them packing; we, the squirrel hunters with long rifles, shooting from the trees, sent them packing; you can never beat the squirrel hunters; look at Viet Nam, they didn't send us packing, they didn't even try, they kept up the pressure until the last helicopter left the embassy in Saigon.
And now, here we are again fighting the squirrel hunters, the Kuwait thing, I suppose that was good; we went in and threw Sadam out, then we left, maybe that was good. But now, the fighting in Iraqi, all that frightful war, for not much of anything, and now we are in Afghanistan the British and the Russians couldn't quell them, so are we? I have attempted to read some of the history of this collision, of proper faith and the others. In 1921 Winston Churchill, in a speech to the House of Commons spoke:

" - - - - at the head of whom the chief Bin Suad maintains himself. This Arab chief has long been in a state of warfare, raid and reprisal with King Hussein and with his neighbours generally. A large number of Bin Saud's followers belong to the Wahabi sect, a form of Mohammedanism which bears, roughly speaking, the same relation to orthodox Islam as the most militant form of Calvinism would have borne to Rome in the fiercest times of the religious wars. The Wahabis profess a life of exceeding austerity, and what they practice themselves they religiously enforce on others. They hold it as an article of duty, as well as of faith, to kill all those who do not share in their opinions - - - - "

This was almost a hundred years ago and the situation has become worse, not better.
Well, what do I know? Come in this room, my private room for most cases; come in here."
And he showed Sam a small room with a lap top, printer and whatever else. A work room for Dave, with a little flap covered hole where he could look out and see people who wanted to register. Lots of shelves with lots of books and papers.
"I am writing about my time in the army; all this stuff is about my time and the history that went before it. I am writing it; it is already over eight hundred pages, perhaps its only my thoughts, but,

one day I would like to see it in bindings, maybe just for me."
Sam said.
"If I stayed over tomorrow, would you let me read a section or two?"
"I hoped you would ask me that.
It covers my time in the Middle East; my whole career, my working life, I think of my time there and I wonder whether I would have been a better human as a wall street broker or a bank person. But that's what is left so I'm writing about it. In my time there were two people who opened their arms to me; well, sort of, two women.
In Iraqi it was Jena Asghar she ran a sort of youth club / library / hangout / place to hide / in Mosul; she founded it with a sort of protestor man. Well they ran it together for a year or so, then he disappeared, she didn't know what happened to him then or later. By the time she had figured out that he would not be back, she was running the place on her own. So, I happened on to her from a small boy I knew of who needed helping. There was no connection, no romantic, nothing; I just showed up when I could and helped with the children. I brought food and clothing but most of all I taught an English class and the majority of the children took part; so that was my part in all of this. We went on like this for almost two years, and more and more I grew to admire Jena; she

was devoted to the Iraqi children and more and more came; they almost all had at least one parent missing so this was a place for them to be at peace, at much as peace was there. But then the army decided me for other work and I was sent back stateside. I said goodbye to the kids and to Jena; but you know, she never said anything affectionate or sort of loyal, she just said goodbye. I gave her five thousand dollars when I left, but she never wrote or phoned; why do you think that was?"

Dave reached for another beer and gave me a grin.

"And then in Afghanistan there was Afsoon Ahwari, not the same sort of person at all. I was there working away at my army works, living more or less like I do now; work in the day, reading and a couple of glasses of wine at night, just hanging out for my time really. One day my major came by and said the colonel had noticed in my papers from Iraqi about my time with the children, he asked if I could do something the same there. I said I could. So, in a couple of days' time I was called to the colonel's office to meet the person I was to help.

That was Afsoon Ahwari. She was different from Jena; Afsoon was about, well, I don't know, somewhere in her forties. She ran an establishment providing help to all kind of people, but what she wanted help for was a group of people, all sorts of people, who wanted to learn English. I said I would go and have a look and decide what would be good. The next night I went and met her and she took me to this group; all kinds, young kids, women, some men all willing and ready to learn. The room had a wall painted yellow, I asked if Afsoon could get it painted white, she said tomorrow. Then I talked to the class about what they knew. OK, I told Afsoon and the class, there will be a class on Tuesdays and Wednesdays, the first class the day after tomorrow, class will be from six until nine. And I said I'll see you then.

For each class I would type out a list of English stuff, all different kinds of stuff but with some progress in content and vocabulary; I printed out copies for the class and I had my lap top with a projector to show the stuff on the wall.

It was very hard, focusing on that stuff for that bunch of students for two or three hours. Each night my shirt and jeans were wet with sweat and I wore a headband so I could see.

But, progress was made. One night, Afsoon brought my colonel and major to attend class and they were happy. At the next class Afsoon came and waited, when class was over, she said.

"Come, come and have tea with me."

She put out the lights and we went to a quiet little room away from all else. She sat me down and went to make tea, she came back with some tea, tea like I never had before, it soothed and brought a feeling of peace, my wet shirt and jeans didn't matter anymore. We sat and talked about the class, some of the people had come to her and told her how much they were learning. She gave me more tea, I was relaxed. She said she was distressed a bit, that the class took so much of me that my shirt was wet long before the end. I told her that was OK and I went home to shower after the class. She still said it was wearing after every class; she got up and walked over behind me and gave me a wonderful massage across my shoulders. Most nights after class, we talked into the night and she made that special tea; but no hopes for the future, but no fears for it either. But then my time was up and I left, no more tea, no more Afsoon, but I'm here, writing about that time, trying to remember.

The next day Sam settled down after breakfast to read sections of Dave's work. By lunchtime he told Dave it was an absorbing tale and he was ready to read it when it first was printed.

"But I'm going to keep after you to keep after it. You here?"

Dave said he would keep on going and smiled as Sam and Jess left.

Chapter 23.—Interlude.

Choosing each stone, and poising every weight,
Trying the measures of breadth and height;
down, and there erecting new,
Founding a firm state by proportions true.
Andrew Marvell
The First Anniversary of the government under Oliver Cromwell.

It was less than an hour to the marina and Jess and Sam got there about ten. They pulled down the drive which was good but not any new surface, but when they got down to the upper level, they saw the marina had wire fenced its land, from the adjacent farmland, and there were hens, ducks, geese and two pig sties there.
"So, what do you think of that Jess? A bit of a farm belonging to the marina."
They drove down to park the car and got out to have a look and a sniff and see how it was after all this time.
They walked down to Joy and Olive's boat and tapped on the coming, Olive's head poked out, and she said.

"Oh, Sam and Jess, how lovely to see you, come on board, oh come and see us."
Sam lifted Jess down and stepped down himself; he got a long hug from Olive and then another hug from Joy.
"So, you're all right then," he said, laughing, "the marina is still here and doing well by what I saw on the way in."
Olive motioned them inside and Joy put the kettle on. Olive said.
"There have been little things since you left, things to make it better to live here; Joy and I have become farmers, you saw the field as you came in; we provide cheap range eggs for Matvei to sell here at the marina, also cheap range ducks and geese and we have two pigs growing fat and we have two steers mixed in with the farmer's little herd; all those for the marina Sam, so Matvei and Olga have lots to do, besides the weekly delivery you set up before you left. There are other things, but you will see them as you visit the other sailors. But what of you? Are you well?"
"Yes, Jess and I are all right. I'm married to Nina and we have two little girls, I'm working at what I did when I was here, Nina is now an accomplished artist and fills her time with that. You remember Val? Well she is part of the company I work for; she is very happy too. I'm here as a part of a break in work, Nina sent me."

Sam drank his tea and said he was going to visit some of the other sailors. But before he left he asked them.
“So, who is in charge here now?”
Olive grinned, “Joy and I are.”
He rambled along the dock, remembering all the events that led the boat owners here, he saw a tousled head.
“Hey Dave, what are you repairing today?”
Dave came out looking for whoever was calling.
“Well, that’s a surprise for us to see you again, here among your tribe, come on aboard, and Jess too, Hobo has not many friends like him.”
Jess got carried into the cockpit and looked around for Hobo, and he climbed out too and the old ‘around the cockpit chase’ took place again, with Dave and Sam sitting with their feet up watching their pets with delight.”
“Hobo is older now,” said Dave, “he will slow down quicker than he used to, but the old friends played together as before, but now with more lasting interest than previously, with more friendliness.” So, they played, leaving their men to talk.
“Can you keep busy with your work here?” Asked Sam.
“I have lots to do for the boat people, the propane work keep me a bit busy, there are three cars here

now and I look after them, keep them running, get the MOT inspection done; so, I keep busy."
"Do you have any friends since I left?"
Dave smiled, "there is a lady I met in the village, she keeps bees and ferrets, believe it or not, so we meet and I do whatever is needed on her house and we have an evening together. Hobo likes it there, likes the smells I suppose, but that's all - - - for him, that's all."
"Olive tells me that she and Pat are sort of running things. How does that work out?"
"Oh, very well, they love to have things straight without making other people do it; everyone here is very happy with their work."
"I still have my boat," said Sam, " moored against our dock, Val's boat is there too, but a bit like ours at the moment, we look after them but we haven't used them for a bit; but we intend to, even if for a weekly cruise, something, because our boats were the start of all that we have."
"So, you still see Val?" asked Dave.
"Oh yes, we work together with my old boss Arnold, so I see the both of them every week. She still the same, fun to work together and to be with but she doesn't have much to say about her life."
"About her life," mused Dave, "she told me a bit about her life once; how she came to be here with Francis. Her father owned the boat, you know, and she and her father went sailing a lot, so they

were together they lived a life shared by time on the boat. Then her father met a woman; he wanted to spend time with her; so, he gave Val the boat and she went on and learned to sail it on her own. They were still close, she and her father, at home, doing other things; but Val didn't spend much time with Blanca, the woman who came to be her stepmother. But even this was, well, not OK, but tolerable. Then, well, she didn't tell me; but I think she was seduced or accosted, or something; but she found she was pregnant with Francis. She didn't tell me what she thought about the baby or why ever she wanted to have it then, I never knew that part. She told her father she wanted money and she would leave him with whatever people he had with Blanca and her sons. She did have money from her dad, not too much, but enough to live on a boat, she went away on the boat before her father knew she was pregnant. I don't know where she went in her final days, but she made it to a hospital and Francis was born. She went back to her boat with Francis. She finished up here and, well, you know the rest; but she is a bit strange about all of her past. But I believe she is a very good mother and whatever past she has with her father is long gone."

"She comes quite often to our home," said Sam, "Francis plays with our girls, even if they are so much younger, quite often they stay on her boat and often they stay at our house for dinner. But, like you, I don't know much about her, but we all like her and she is our friend. So, we enjoy her and feels happy when she is with us."

Sam and Jess spent more time with Dave, talking about the marina and the people who lives there; Sam still getting the unfamiliar feeling that he no longer belonged here. Sam told Dave that he wanted to visit some other of the people and he went on his way.

He went to visit Arthur, of the ancient wooden boat and perhaps Nancy, the Long Island lady who came to be a part of his life when Sam was there.

Sam banged on Arthur's hull; a face emerged.

"Sam and Jess, what a nice surprise! Come on board, come in."

Sam and Jess got on board and Duke the Greyhound welcomed them, and then Nancy looked out with a smile.

"Sam, come on in and have a coffee with us, come in please, it is so nice to see you again, we thought you had gone forever."

They sat and chatted, ate Nancy's home-made scones and Sam told them about Nina and the girls, their lives together in the house given to them by Guiudre.

Arthur explained their lives at the marina.

"We still have our own slips and our two boats, we live like you see us here, no set pattern, we are in one boat while the other is getting cleaned, just use them like a house maybe. But we go on two cruises now; each year. We take Nancy's boat in the spring and go off to a place that is, well, somewhere one of us wants to go; last spring we went south and cruised for a couple of months in the rivers of Georgia, most of the time in lonely places or anchored among small communities; we liked that very much and it wetted our appetite for more cruises, so last fall we drifted around the outer banks and got back for Thanksgiving here. So, we share and have a lot of fun in our boats in our marina that you gave to us."

"It is a good thing you have met each other," said Sam, "it is a very good thing to have people rely on you and you with them. It makes me want to go home to my family; so, I'll visit Matvei and Olga and go home."

Sam and Jess strolled along the dock; but there was no reply from their boat; so he walked up to their store but was not fully prepared for the changes that had taken place. Olga was behind the counter and rushed out to hug him when she knew who he was.

"Sam and Jess, after all this time, are you here for a visit? Here to stay, where is your boat? Where is Nina?"

Sam visited Matvie and Olga but again the growth of their business and the manner in which they did all the connection with their people in the marina and the way in which they grasped the things needed to bring it all together, made him realize that his time at the marina was past.
He shook their hands and he and Jess left. Sam was glad to leave, to head homeward.
He got to the motel and went to sign in again, looking forward to being able to read Dave's history. He was at the check in place, outside Dave's peep hole but nobody came. He waited a few moments and another door opened and a woman came in; a woman with dark skin and even darker eyes; she looked at Sam, puzzled. Sam looked back at her, then smiled.
"You're Afsoon the tea lady."
She looked back, beginning to bristle.
"And who are you?"
"Dave and I shared some beers on my way down, he promised me a read of some of his history if I came in on my way home."
"Humf," she said, "well, he's in the shower," then she grinned, " well you know a bit about me, so come on in."
Sam went in and Jess gave Afsoon a sniff and settled at Sam's feet.
"Well," Afsoon said, smiling broadly "you can see he married me in Afghanistan; it was a hard time,

he couldn't really stay with me there and it was probably impossible for me to move here, unless he married me. So, he did, and here I teach Eastern Studies at a college and," she grinned, "come here weekends to drink wine and make him tea."

"Any massages?" Said Sam straight-faced.

But then Dave came in and the exchange of their history changed to 'how are you' again and all that stuff.

Sam had a shower and spent the evening with Afsoon and Dave, just drifting from one subject to another ,family lives, dogs, writing, Sam had a discussion, or a lecture perhaps, on his historic statement the Afghanistan's importance was a strategic means to block access to India from others, mostly Russia, she leaned on this and gave her views on the Afghanistan's view of all this; but it was a pleasant evening and Sam and Jess went for a walk before going to bed.

The next day was a 'rest day' for Sam, he got up late and then went to Dave for a section of his history to read. He read most of the afternoon and took it back to Dave. He smiled.

"I love your views of the history and the military decisions that were made and lost by all parties trying to control the country; what must be in some other section of your history," he grinned,

"is your analysis of what kind of peace there might be and what kind of peace that might be"
Dave smiled wryly.
"The only peace that there will ever be is one where the Wahabi controls everything, that's what I think."
Sam took his hand.
"Good luck with that Dave, anyway, I'll be up early and won't see you then.
Goodbye to you and goodbye to Afsoon when she gets home again."
Sam and Jess left about five-thirty and headed home with hopes high. He now knew that his life and his loves were there in Giuirde's old home, now is and his family. He thought of Nina, Alexis and Amelia. He pondered Arnold, Val and their binding together of their company-which-is-not-a-company. He sped on the best way home, he stopped for Jess but hurried on.
He drew into the gate at about three and, lo-and-behold, his family was there to meet him and Jess.
That night he lay in Nina's arms and said sleepily.
"This river bend of Giuidre's is my home, my home; and all I want is here."

Chapter 24.—Sam's Renascence

O litel book, thou art so unconning,
How darst thou put thy-self in preces for drede
Geoffrey Chaucer. The Flower and the Leaf.

That night, on this day of his renascence, in Nina's arms, he told her.

"With all my heart, my life here exceeds any and all my expectations, here; with you, Amelia and Alexis, Chassie, the dogs, the walks along the river, the boat; what more could I want? I just want our lives to grow for everybody, just everybody, not just the girls growing up, but you in your world of art," Sam giggled into her ear, "I love it when you are wrapped up in your work, you are most attractive to me all painted up and absorbed."

Nina turned to him and smiling said.

"Do you want to try for girl number three now?"

"No, I love what we have, and can focus on them, I think more could sort of diminish what we have to give. No, what we have is enough. But we could practice tonight to make sure we could do it."

And they did.

And after that Sam lay holding Nina's hand and drifted off to sleep, in swirling clouds of pale blue and Brie cheese colored clouds, he saw sleeping images of all the things he told Nina about, drifting pictures of their favorite things, special, places, the growing childhood lives; slowly the pale blue turned darker, and the Brie turned a deeper bronze, and the images grew faint, and he fell asleep.

When he awoke, Nina was gone, when he went for breakfast, he was the only one there, but in his very satisfied state of mind, he decided to indulge in a special breakfast alone and made coffee, fried bacon, eggs, fried bread and fried banana and took it outside to Giuildre's place in the sun by the garden shed and permitted himself this lonesome and private time.

Later, inside he went up to Nina's art room to say hello. He got a kiss and then she told him the one of the air-conditioning vents in the ceiling of her room did not work anymore.

"All right," Sam said, "perhaps the vent has come off the fitting, I'll get a couple more clips and go and see."

He got his stuff and lowered the attic ladder and went on up. He shouted down.

"The hose is not attached to the vent; I'll make it right".

As he finished his work and made to go back down, he saw a cardboard box under the eaves far from the ladder. He made his way over, lifted it up and carried it over to the stepladder, and downstairs, he carried the box back out to Giuidre’s sun seat and opened it to look inside; mostly it was papers and documents long out of date, but right at the bottom were three exercise books, they had Giuidre’s writing on the cover. He put two to one side and read the first. He read of the river, the river walk; and the plants there, in the bank or in the water. He laid that aside and picked up one of the others, and finally the last one.

He sat and looked in the distance at nothing, then picked them up and went to see Nina.

“Love, do you have a minute to talk?”

“OK’, she said and wiped her brush, “not another proposal of undying love or anything like that?”

Sam smiled.

“No, that’s for tonight. This is very different. In the box I brought down from the attic there were three little books, handwritten by Giuidre sometime in the past. One is called “Tales from the Riverway”, and is all about what young people might see on the river, the next is called “River Bank Tales” and the last is called “Creatures on the River Plants. They have a full text and a layout, there are descriptions of what the story is about, but there are no illustrations. I think you must take the time and read them and perhaps think about finishing them.

So, here they are for you to read; and I had better do some work for Arnold."
They met for dinner outside; the girls, the dogs, hamburgers and hot dogs, orange juice for the children and red wine for the parents.
"Will you come with me up the river bank." Asked Sam.
"yes, yes." Shouted Alexis and Amelia, joined by excitement from the two dogs, Nina said she would come and they all set off together.
As they walked Nina said she had read the story books of Giuidre and said she didn't think she wanted to work on them. Sam said nothing; but he wondered about that; such a chance to do something to remember Giuirdre, but he walked on with the girls and the dogs enjoying the evening there with his family.
When the girls were bathed, told stories and tucked up in bed, and the dogs were settled down in their beds Nina came over and sat in his lap, she put her arms around him and buried her face in his neck.
"I will make illustrations for Giuirdre's books. When I read them, I could hear her voice reading to me; I didn't like it, not then; but now I feel better about it; I'll make special time to work on them, do a goodbye for her, one she would have been proud of."

Nina didn't begin work on Giuidre's books, not for a while; she thought about the books, what Giuidre thought about when she wrote them, about her own daughters, what they thought about them. She went for a walk along the river bank, all on her own, to try to feel what Giuidre felt when she wrote, at last she sat on Giuidre's summer seat, like Giuidre did when Sam made it for her, and at last she decided. Late afternoon, before the girls finished school, she bought a bottle of wine out to Giuidre's summer seat and called Sam to join her, as he sat down and poured two glasses of wine; he then settled down to wait for what he had been brought there to be briefed on. But it was nothing to do with the girls, or anything to do with the house, no, nothing to do with any plans Nina had been thinking of, no, nothing like that.

So, Nina told him her plan.

"Nina said she had decided what to do about "Guiudre's River Walk" books; we must produce books that reflect our feeling for these books on our life.

I will illustrate each page: each insect, each butterfly, each toad, the places the insects live will be real, the story from one page to the next must be clear.

But we must be a part of making the books; so, throughout the books there will be double pages

paintings of the people making the books. The girls will be there commenting on the illustrations of the insects and animals, they will vote on the paintings where each insect or animal lives. You and Jess and Tina must be woven into the texture of each picture. So, each book will grow in this way until all three are finished until all of us are satisfied. That is how the books will be made."
Sam thought about all this and played with his glass of wine.
"It's a big task for you, not only the illustrations, but the family paintings you will add, it's a big job and I think it will take two months; and you remember how hard you had to work to get the texture of the material how you wanted it? But I think it's a wonderful plan, I'll do anything I can to help you; this is the kind of thing I had in mind; the idea of having the children involved is lovely. It will be a fine thing for us to leave behind for Giuirdre.
You know the publisher that printed the first book you did, he had lots of nice ideas, you should call him, not to influence, what you produce, but publishing ideas that can influence what books you make. You should be aware that your 'Giuidre's River Walk" might become a big success. Wait and see."
Nina thought about Amelia and Alexis, and Tina to help the search, about Sam and Jess who might

help sometimes. She made a plan of how to get it done; she needed help and that was the first thing she went about.
She told Sam.
"I'm going to get some help from a photographer, there will be lots of images of flowers, insects, other animals for the girls to study; need someone who will be a part of things with us; I'm going to see Aksel Hansen, he did the photos for the children's Christmas Pagaent, I expect he will understand.
She drove on quietly, still thinking about about Giuidre's Books.
Aksel lived in a lonely house up a leaf covered lane, Nina liked to visit, just for the experience of being there among the leaves and the animals that played there, so different from the other roads and footpaths. She parked by Aksel's gate and walked in, greeted by Aksel's two Red Setters she sat on her heals for licking and head rubbing. Aksel came out and gave her a hand to pull on and she got up and gave him a hug as well.
"Well, what do I owe this meeting for?"
His English was good, he knew what everything was called, but he still jumbled up some of the phrases when he was at ease.
Nina grinned.
"I'm starting on a project that will be in honor of Giuidre. Sam found three exercise books and

Giuidre had written three children's tales about walking on the riverbank. I have decided to complete the books by painting the insects and creatures that the children see but also, I want to include paintings of the children looking at the grass and other plants. It will be a long project to produce three publishing books and not get the children fed up with their part in making it.
I want you to help with photos; for each book I plan to look at ten areas of grass, with the children, and I want an eight by ten photograph taken by you of each area; I want an 11 by 14 print, one color and one black and white of each area; I want two sets, one to keep and one to work on. But when we bring the children to see what we can capture and the photos will show what we want when we draw and paint each area for the book. While the children and I are looking at the things in the grass I want you to take 35mm shots of the girls and the dogs poking around being childish so on the intermediate pages there will be images of a young family examining the grasses. That is the project. I want your help in taking the photos, making prints and your thoughts on the results. Will you help me?"
"Of course, I'll help, it will be a pleasure."
"Your name will be in the credits when it is published."

So, Aksel got out his ancient 8X10 camera, tripod, film holders and made a list of all that he did not have and they made an appointment in a week's time to meet at Nina's house to do the first two areas.

Nina went away with joy in her heart for having Aksel to help her.

She got out the children's book she had illustrated before and sat down with Alexis and Amelia to show them how it was made and then to show them the exercise books with the new books and to tell them how they were going to make new books but the new books would have photographs of them inside, she told them how a photographer was going to come and explore the footpath and share with them all the insects and animals, photograph them so the three of them can make stories of the animals. Nina took them on river-walk trips on nice days to practice what they would do for their book.

So, the day came and together with Aksel and Lina they set off on their walk, at the first area Aksel put up the tripod and the camera, he looked to Nina who said.

"Take the photos first so we shall look at the real photo."

When Aksel was done Nina sat with the girls and Lina and studied the insects there: climbing the stalks of grass, hiding under leaves, all different

kinds. Nina encouraged the girls to make up names for the living things they saw, she made a note for when they composed their story.
They went home and Nina said she would come to Aksel's tomorrow to pick up the prints.
For the next two weeks Nina worked alone, bringing in the girls to see what she had done; she was setting the book for the material that would come from the other areas but also preparing the book for the stories the girls would write, later.
All the characters would, eventually, need names; she made up a few as she went along, but reserved the right for the girls to change them when the time came:
"Columbus the caterpillar, foufou the feeling ant, early the earwhig, cilla the centipede" and so on.
Nina would sit in a team with the girls one each side and they would look at Nina's works: the finished art for the book subjects, they talked about the story Nina was making and they argued about the story for children. The children's ideas for the stories were much different to hers and Nina knew that their stories would sit better in the art world she would provide, she paid strict attention to their reasons for the story they wanted, she realized that their background for their choices was real in their world.

Later, when Nina's work was about 80% complete; she decided to show the publisher, she made an appointment and drove down one morning.
She met the same art director and the publisher that she had worked with on her (now famous) children's book of long ago.
"We wanted to meet you again." Said the publisher. "your last book was so good we wanted to know about this project."
Nina explained about finding the three exercise books written in the past by Giuidre and he decision to make them into some kind of memorium to Giuidre's kindness to all who knew her, "particularly us". She was using the text Giuidre had left behind, but decided that intersperses of paintings of the children as they investigated the grassy areas would add to the value of the book and lead young readers to the stories that the children have written and will write.
Then she folded out the pages she had painted of the insects and animals.
Then she told between the photographs of the insects, the interspersed paintings of the children and Lina looking at the pages as they were being drawn and the children writing their little stories.
I intend to have three story books, all the same and a nice painted cardboard folder with animals and bits of the story.

So, that's my plan. I wondered what you thought of it and what guidance you could give me."
Well, to Nina's delight there followed a day of does and don'ts "this paper or that paper, font type and size, colors to use and not use, pictures of the children to emphasize the age of the story and a promise for a contract very soon. So, with her valise full of things to remember and her valued book and her mind full of compliments, she drove home in high dudgeon with a special bottle of wine to share with Sam.

Chapter 26 Nina's Book & The Growth of the Gallery.

There is no way to success in our art
but to take off your coat,
grind paint, and work like a digger on the railroad,
all day and every day.
Ralph Waldo Emerson.
Conduct of Life

There was six months of Nina and the children working away at their book; Nina was surprised that the girls kept at it, she supposed it was the changing of the stories and the new characters they introduced, so Nina was able to maintain a decent rate of progress.

Sam, outside of all of this, except as an occasional spectator and pillow talk, thought again about a plan he had considered before but abandoned it then because it seemed not in line with their other lives and work. But now it seemed to him that the time had come again. He always thought Nina and some of her painting acquaintances would enjoy and to good things if they could have an art gallery all of their own; he had visions of shows, a place to have shows by beginning artists, show of their own work, wine evenings, chamber music with shows, canapes and new wine, maybe poetry readings; the gallery would be the center of a new and vibrant life. He thought. Well, he thought about lots of things but not necessarily that they would think of, but he had fond hopes of a sort of "staff room" where all the artists meet and do the things they do now: discussing portraits, work, techniques and what-ever was in their minds. The staff room would not be in the public area and would be for the artists an enclave for their privacies and their hopes. He felt this way for a long while, but the chance to talk to Nina about it, but now the time seemed right.

He drove down on Friday night, the night the artists gathered; not all of them came each week but he thought a cadre would be enough to test his proposal.

When he got there, he apologized.

"I'm here, unbidden representing Nina's family with a proposal. I have thought about it but I never found the way to talk to Nina about it. So, while she is absorbed in her publishing work, I thought I would come down and try it on you lot.

"I want to suggest that you group of artists have a gallery here, or near here. A gallery where you could have shows: young artists, groups of artists etc. there could be wine evenings with chamber music, poetry readings, there would be a staff room, like this room where you could have the private discussions you have now. Well, you could do whatever you wanted; I thought it could bring a new purpose to your work, anyway, that's my thought. You could form a little company to own the building, you would each be directors, with a chief elected once a year. There is a building the next street over, an old animal feed store, it has two floors and a basement, you would need central air etc, but it could be nice; painted in gallery colors etc. That's my suggestion. I'm sure that crowd-funding would provide most of what is needed. Oh, I drifted into this idea while I was considering a gallery for Nina, but this sounds like much more fun.

Well, that's what I came for, I'll go off home, let me know if you have any interest."

Nina and the girls worked a bit each day on the third book, but it still took four months to get it done; when it was done Nina folded it in a valise and they took it to the publisher. Nina had a fine time with the editor and one of the younger ladies took the girls for ice cream. They all had a fine time and they set off home to see Sam. On the way Nina stopped and bought some treats and they got home and told him how much the publisher liked the book and how the ice cream was very good; and Sam understood how their triumph was good for all of them. Nina took the girls up with Chassie and came back dressed only in her best dressing gown and with the bag of goodies and a new bottle of wine; the goodies were two bagels with cream and smoked salmon on them and two large wine glasses. She opened the dressing gown and had nothing on underneath.

"(I know you can have it warm in here, she said)' as she locked the cabin door saying.

"I know we have spent a lot of time on the book; so here is a chance to make it up a bit."

So; each had two bagels with smoked salmon and a half bottle of wine later and Sam cuddled up with Nina she said.

"Well, what have you been up to all this time?"

Although he had planned to keep silent for a while, Sam thought this was a nice time to tell her about his project for her.

"Well, I have a long story to tell you. I had thought for a long time that you should have some more outlet for your talents. I thought it would be OK for you to have a gallery to show works that you like, for young artists etc., but I always thought it could be a bigger thing that you would want some of the time, so I gave up the idea. Then, about a month ago I went to your Friday art-group meeting; I told them I was there under secondment. But what I told them that I was there to suggest that they had a gallery. All of them, as a group. I suggested a gallery where they could display art of various kinds, your own art, poetry readings, wine parties, a staff room where you could all meet and discuss art the way you do; a venue for you all to take part for whatever you want, just all kinds of things. You lot would be the directors of the gallery; it would be your world. I asked what they thought and then I left. Since then they said they liked the idea and then I bought the house for the gallery. When I looked into it, I found the town owned the house for some back, taxes from years ago. They were anxious to get rid of it and I bought it cheap and I have been getting crowd funded from businesses and Tom who did our house is working on it. I had planned for it to be a surprise but this way is better. You will be a director and I hope you will enjoy being part of it."

Nina pondered.

"A gallery?"

"Yes, we can go down tomorrow and you can look at it."

"Oh, Sam, what a wonderful idea, you spoil me, what can I do? Do you need a third daughter?"

"You keep saying that to me – 'a third daughter' do you want one?"

"Oh, you keep spoiling me again! Of course, I want one, come here and I'll explain it all to you."

And with all the time spent on her book project and Sam's immersion in his gallery project, there seemed to be lots of time for Nina to show him, and the time went on, and on, the next morning Sam said it was time to dress and they would go for breakfast before they went to the gallery. And so, with crisp bacon, strong coffee they went on to the gallery; Nina was anxious and excited, with all her art-friends knowing about it.

Sam pulled into the small parking lot and they looked at the outside; it looked finished.

"Tom worked on the outside first, said Sam, " he power washed the siding and then your art group decided what colors to paint it. I was surprised at their choice, well, at first, I was surprised but then as time passed, I liked the effect and now I like it very much. The gold color of the siding sets off the plum color of the trim and the gold of the trim makes it look sort of royal. Well, anyway that's what it is for now. Come on in and we can see what rooms there are and what sort of use we have thought of. Tom decided to make a clean start; he sanded all the wood floors and varnished them to a fine finish; before he started; he took the staircase out and vacuum blasted it with soda to clean it all and that is varnished to show off.

The color of the rooms was all selected by your art-friends.
That room is to be your staff room where you can all meet in private, over there will be the kitchen, that corner will have heavy drapes to go around the back when you have a chamber orchestra playing there. And upstairs there are four room where you can have multiple shows if you want. It's a very nice old building, it was once a feed store. So, you will be a director of the group that owns it. You art-people have to create a corporation to own the building, as soon as I have the finances straight I shall sell it to you. You will all be equal owners.
What do you think Nina?"
"It's lovely. I can't stop thinking about all we can do here, and it will be another avenue for thought and art; besides what we have all done so far."
"And you might have to look after Number three by then."
And so; another child coming (something they both wanted), the gallery to get Nina out of the house more. A broader social move for Nina and leaving Sam to sit with Jess down on Leia to make little plans for Arnold's Company.
The gallery seemed to Sam to be a fitting end to the 'picked-up" of his life with Nina; it always seemed to be a life they had drifted into: buying Leia so cheap, meeting Giuidre and having their

lives together, then joined by Nina, then Jess and Tina, then the loss of Giuidre and their period of being alone. But now Nina had created an art-life that was very good for her, they had the girls and were going to have another. So that life had drifted away, and a new one had come along; and it seemed to be formed by the gallery and all the plans that everybody had.

The life continued, and Sam pondered those plans: the growing up of the children, Nina's art-world, one day sailings on Liela with a crew of kids, Jess and Nina growing older, bed in the aft cabin with Nina – for ever!

The future seemed good with Giuidre's memories.

www.ingramcontent.com/pod-product-compliance
Lightning Source LLC
LaVergne TN
LVHW010546160826
845677LV00013B/3016